D1520593

INVESTMENT MANAGEMENT AND MISMANAGEMENT
HISTORY, FINDINGS, AND ANALYSIS

Innovations in Financial Markets and Institutions

Editor:
Mark Flannery
University of Florida

Other books in the series:

INVESTMENT MANAGEMENT AND MISMANAGEMENT
HISTORY, FINDINGS, AND ANALYSIS

Seth C. Anderson, Ph.D., CFA
University of North Florida

🍃 Springer

Library of Congress Control Number: 2006924635

Anderson, Seth C.
  Investment management and mismanagement: history, findings, and analysis
          p.cm. (Innovations in financial markets and institutions ; 17)
  Includes bibliographical references, endnotes and index.

ISBN-13: 978-0387-33829-3   e-ISBN-13: 978-0387-33830-9
ISBN-10: 0-387-33829-2   e-ISBN-10: 0-387-33830-6   Printed on acid-free paper.

Printed in the United States of America.

9 8 7 6 5 4 3 2 1

springeronline.com

DEDICATION

To my wife Linda

ACKNOWLEDGEMENT

The author wishes to express appreciation to Professor Mark Flannery of the University of Florida, who supported the proposal to undertake this work, and to Judith Pforr at Springer, who worked patiently for many months. The completion of the book was greatly facilitated by the word processing of Katia Ushakova and the editorial work of Linda Anderson.

CONTENTS

PREFACE

Concomitant with the growth of personal wealth in the United States over the past 150 years, there has arisen the opportunity for wealth holders to invest their monies in a variety of assets. These investment assets basically comprise real assets, stocks, and bonds, which are the primary components of most portfolios managed by either individual or institutional investors.

This book presents the reader with: (1) a brief overview of investment management and its historical evolution, (2) the findings of a substantial amount of academic research into the performance of investment managers, (3) the various issues associated with both institutional and individual portfolio mismanagement, (4) the impact of investment costs and the issue of mismanagement, and (5) a treatment of the constructs of suitability and churning. The articles referenced are primarily works from academic journals, including: *The Journal of Finance*, *Journal of Financial Economics*, and others, as well as from practitioner-oriented venues, such as *Financial Analyst Journal* and various law journals. This work will be of value to both academic and legal researchers and to students as a convenient source of summarized studies in these areas, while practitioners will find value in it as an efficient reference for determining both the benefits and pitfalls of individual and professional investment management.

Ides of March, 2006

I: INTRODUCTION

The purpose of this introduction is to provide the reader with a chapter-by-chapter overview of this book. This may be beneficial because the format of each chapter varies widely, depending upon the topic.

Chapter II lays out the investment process, which involves both the investor and the investment manager. An investor has a particular objective of which the attainment is the responsibility of the manager. How well the manager performs in this regard ultimately determines the manager's evaluation.

Chapter III presents the historical backdrop of today's environment in which the manager must function. The three most important investment-related entities of interest on this stage are: the stock exchange, investment banking, and investment companies.

Chapter IV presents two opposing schools of thought pertaining to the value of active investment management. The efficient market theorists claim that security prices always fully reflect all available information. In contrast, the traditionalist camp contends that informed traders can earn a return on their activity of information-gathering. Centered in this controversy are multiple issues of anomalies. One of these anomalies, addressed in Chapter V, is the value of analysts' recommendations.

Abridgements of various studies relating to investment management largely constitute the remaining chapters of this book. Chapter VI involves the issues of mutual fund performance, market timing, and performance persistence. Chapter VII comprises findings of studies in the area of individual investor performance. Subsequently, Chapter VIII considers the impact of investment costs on portfolio returns and the issue of investment mismanagement.

Chapters IX and X provide in-depth treatments of the issues of suitability and churning, which are frequently matters of concern in the numerous investment-related lawsuits and arbitration complaints that appear in today's investment world. The final chapter of the book, Chapter XI, provides a summary of the findings of the above chapters. Now let us proceed to Chapter II for a discussion of the overall investment process.

II: THE INVESTMENT PROCESS

2.1 Introduction

An investment portfolio may be managed by the individual portfolio owner or by a chosen professional manager, such as a mutual fund, trust department, or other financial entity. Regardless of which alternative is selected, the investment process, as diagrammed in Figure 2.1, is relatively straightforward. As is seen, this process encompasses the portfolio owner, the portfolio

Figure 2.1: The Investment Process

The Portfolio Owner
Objectives   Risk Tolerance   Tax Status   Investment Horizon
↓
The Portfolio Manager's Responsibilities
Step 1. Asset Allocation
Stocks   Bonds   Real Assets
Domestic   or   Non-domestic
Step 2. Security Selection
Based on Cash Flows, Comparables, Technical, and Other Information
Which Stocks? Which Bonds? Which Real Assets?
Step 3. Trade Execution
Impact of Commission, Bid/Ask Spread, and Price Pressure
Trade Frequency   Trade Size
↓
The Manager's Performance
What return did the portfolio manager make?
How much risk did the manager take?
Did the manager underperform or outperform?

manager, and the manager's performance, to each of which we now respectively turn our attention.

2.2 The Portfolio Owner

As shown in Figure 2.1, the portfolio owner's needs and wishes are a direct function of the owner's: (1) objectives, (2) utility function, (3) tax issues, and (4) investment horizon. Some owners are better suited to riskier investments in seeking to achieve their objectives than are others. For certain owners, tax issues may be of paramount importance, and investment horizons obviously differ, depending upon the owners' objectives. Regardless of whether the portfolio is managed by the owner or by a professional manager, the assets comprising the portfolio should be suitable investments. In the preponderance of portfolios, these assets include stocks, bonds, and real assets, or some combination thereof. The charge of the portfolio manager is to appropriately allocate assets into those investment vehicles that are consistent with the needs and wishes of the portfolio owner.

2.3 The Portfolio Manager

Portfolio management may range from passive indexing to a wide variety of active strategies involving security selection, and possibly market timing. The portfolio manager's selection of securities is based on either fundamental or technical analyses that may include cash flow analysis, comparable security analysis, and a wide range of other techniques. The manager may use research from different sources, ranging from the *Wall Street Journal*, to purchased research, to a plethora of other public information. This information's value has been a topic of discussion in the investments arena for decades. Some hold that public information may be useful in outperforming the market overall, while others strongly reject this position. The debate continues apace, as is evident in Chapters IV and V.

Once the security selections have been made, the portfolio manager must execute the buying or selling of the target securities. This execution is of considerable importance because of the direct and indirect costs associated with transactions. These costs include: commissions, the bid-ask spread, and the impact of the transaction on the securities' prices. Obviously, the negative impact of these costs on return performance, as discussed in Chapter VIII, increases with trading frequency and order size. We now turn to the issue of the manager's performance.

2.4 The Manager's Performance

The returns generated by the portfolio manager are of paramount importance to the owner. As is offered in Chapter VI, prior to the mid-1900s the evaluation of return performance was often performed via comparable portfolios. However, with the introduction of modern portfolio theory, there came the formal consideration of risk in the analysis of performance. Over the decades there has been considerable attention paid to various risk-related issues in determining whether or not a manager's performance has been better than would be expected from the market overall or from appropriate sectors thereof. However, there are also numerous other factors within the investment arena that differentially impact the return performance of individual managers and professional managers. These factors include: broker influences, informational resources, commission disparities, economies of scale, and other institutional and market constraints, many of which are addressed in Chapters VI, VII, and VIII. Now that we have briefly reviewed the investments process, an overview of the backdrop for investment management is presented in the next chapter.

III: THE HISTORICAL BACKDROP FOR INVESTMENT MANAGEMENT

3.1 Introduction

This chapter is devoted to three of the most important investment-related entities comprising the backdrop for today's investment management environment: (1) the stock exchange, (2) investment banking,[1] and (3) investment companies. Over the past two centuries these institutions evolved in close conjunction with each other and with other financial intermediaries, and were fundamental in shaping today's financial arena. One of the primary sources for this chapter is *A History of Financial Intermediaries*, by Krooss and Blyn, who present the history of our domestic financial institutions from their origins through the 1960s.

As seen in Table 3.1a on the next page,[2] the banks and insurers were the primary financial intermediaries in our county during the first century after the American Revolution. It was also during this time that: the stock exchanges were formed; American investment banking originated; trust companies prospered; pension plans and credit unions arose; and the first domestic investment companies were born. Of these entities, pension plans, credit unions, and investment companies (as listed in Table 3.1b), are seen to gain relative prominence much later in the country's history. Stock

---

[1] This term refers to both primary investment bankers and houses that focus on mostly retail brokerage.

[2] Adapted from Krooss and Blyn, pp. 93, 122, 216.

exchanges and investment banking are not listed, as they do not intermediate assets in the manner of savings-type institutions.[3]

As we know, the history of our financial institutions is rich, and any given sub-area could well fill many interesting volumes.

Table 3.1a: Assets of Selected Financial Intermediaries: 1836-1912 (Millions of Dollars)

Institution	1836	1860	1870	1880	1890	1912
Commercial Banks	622	851	1781	2517	4601	21822
Mutual Savings Banks	11	149	550	882	1743	4015
Savings & Loans Assn.	-	-	-	-	300	952
Life Insurance Cos.	-	24	270	418	771	4409
General Insurance Cos.	-	81	182	239	352	1001
Credit Unions	-	-	-	-	-	-
Private Pension Plans	-	-	-	-	-	-
Investment Cos.	-	-	-	-	-	-
Total	633	1105	2783	4056	7767	32199

Table 3.1b: Assets of Selected Financial Intermediaries: 1922-1967 (Millions of Dollars) (Billions of Dollars 1940 onward)

Institution	1922	1929	1940	1950	1960	1967
Commercial Banks	47467	66235	67.8B	169.9	258.4	454.6
Mutual Savings Banks	6597	9873	11.9B	22.4	40.6	66.4
Savings & Loans Assn.	2802	7411	5.7B	16.9	71.5	143.8
Life Insurance Cos.	8652	17482	30.8B	64.0	119.6	177.8
General Insurance Cos.	2358	4716	5.1B	13.2	29.4	46.6
Credit Unions	11	42	0.3B	1.0	5.7	12.9
Private Pension Plans	90	500	1.0B	6.5	33.1	71.8
Investment Cos.	110	2988	1.0B	3.4	18.8	44.7
Total	68087	109247	123.6B	297.3	577.1	1018.4

Because of space constraints, the following historical synopses include only limited descriptive information about the stock exchange, investment banking, and investment companies. Herein,

---

[3] Trust companies operated independently prior to their nearly complete absorption by banks in the early 1900s.

we attempt to highlight the pertinent institutional developments that still today impact the investment management environment in which portfolio managers operate. We now turn our attention to these investment-related institutions.

3.2 Stock Exchanges

The first of the investment-related entities with which we are concerned is the stock exchange. The stock exchanges began to be established at the close of the 1700s when the total assets of the banks and insurance companies amounted to about $50 million, or about $10 per capita. Depending upon the source, it is unclear as to whether the Philadelphia or New York exchange was the first to be established. However, because of its greater historical and present-day influences, we focus on the New York Stock Exchange, which began operations in 1792.

The Exchange began with the Buttonwood Tree Agreement under which the 17 subscribers to the Exchange agreed to hold public sales of securities at noon and to "deal in shares for ¼ of 1 percent of the selling price." These brokers also agreed not to trade at the other public auctions operating at that time.[4] The early years saw little activity, as indicated by an approximate daily turnover of 100 shares as late as 1827, which rose to 6000 shares per day by 1835. However, one must remember that activity occurred elsewhere other than on the NYSE.[5] Over the decades the number of securities expanded, as did the number of "calls" per day when trading occurred.

---

[4] Oesterle, et al., 1992, "The New York Stock Exchange and Its Out Moded Specialist System: Can the Exchange Innovate to Survive?" p. 238.

[5] Krooss and Blyn, pp. 56-57.

Tangentially, it should be noted that during this period the financial intermediaries—commercial banks, savings banks, and insurance companies—concentrated on business loans, bonds, and mortgages, and did not participate very much in the equity side of the securities markets. That field of activity was left to the investment bankers (discussed in the next section), as buying stocks was not considered altogether respectable.

As quoted in Krooss and Blyn, during the depression of the late 1830s, *The New York Times* announced, "The New York Stock Exchange as at present managed is little more than an enormous gambling establishment." Although the market's prestige did improve, such progress was continuously interrupted by recession or depression. For many of us today, the matter of securities market gaming conjures up images of the 1920s or the late 1990s. However, Krooss and Blyn reveal that this issue has older manifestations, as seen in an 1853 Hunt's editorial:

> ...there is a large amount of money seeking a regular investment in stocks, which is legitimately passed through the hands of those who have a seat in the board, and the capitalist, in business or out, who has surplus means, may certainly purchase such securities as he shall fancy. But the large array of forces in this department is chiefly supported from the losses of outside speculators. The sumptuous living, and the elegant establishments, are most generally paid for out of the money of those who ought never to have touched the traffic, and for whose permanent prosperity the excitement is as dangerous as the chances of the gaming table... It is notorious that the whole system is chiefly supported from the capital of those who have not a dollar to invest, and who ought never to have attempted the speculation.[6]

---

[6] Kroos and Blyn, p. 85.

Even though stocks were generally not held in high regard by many, this did not apparently impact the success of the reorganization of the Exchange during the 1870s. Share volume increased, localized trading "posts" on the Exchange floor evolved, and the specialist system developed via serendipity. Because of the increased activity and the invention of the stock ticker, the call market was gradually replaced by continuous trading, beginning in 1871. All of these, along with new technologies such as telephones on the exchange floor, transformed the Exchange into a national financial center in anticipation of the coming century.[7]

For the remainder of this section, we focus on two aspects of the Exchange that have most significantly impacted investment management over the past century and continue to do so today, albeit to a lesser degree. These two aspects of interest are commissions and stock transactions as effected by specialists. These two issues have been fundamental to the Exchange, as Jennings and Marsh state:

> The operation of the New York Stock Exchange was historically based upon four interrelated principles or rules, all of them designed to protect the economic position of the members of that exchange (i.e., all of them in "restraint of trade" to some extent). (1) Limited membership and exclusive dealing . . . (2) The prohibition against members executing trades in listed securities off the board . . . (3) The minimum commission schedule, and (4) The uniform commission schedule for all transactions, regardless of size.[8]

---

[7]Oesterle, et al,, p. 279.

[8] Jennings and Marsh, 1987, *Securities Regulation*, pp. 558-559.

We first turn to commissions, and next to the specialists, before concluding with comments.

As seen above and at the first of this section, fixed commissions had been a fundamental aspect of the Exchange since its inception. However, these fixed rate policies were not unnoticed by congressional bodies. For example, the House Committee on Banking and Currency, in a 1913 report known as the Pujo Report, found:

> . . . the present rates to be reasonable, except as to stocks, say, of $25 or less in value, and that the exchange should be protected in this respect by the law under which it shall be incorporated against a kind of competition between members that would lower the service and threaten the responsibility of members. A very low or competitive commission rate would also promote speculation and destroy the value of membership. [9]

In spite of the monopoly power of the exchanges exhibited in the area of commission rates and in a wide variety of other aspects, "the exchanges remained essentially self-regulating and without significant supervision until the adoption of the Securities Exchange Act of 1934."

This commission policy would remain entrenched for nearly forty years until competitive forces largely from institutions took their toll. As of the mid-1970s the SEC had been engaged in detailed study of the commission structure for a decade, which culminated in "the requirement for abolition of fixed rates as of May 1, 1975."[10] We will further touch upon the commission issue

---

[9] Gordon v. New York Stock Exchange, sec.2, p. 3.

[10] Ibid., sec.1, p.2

in the section on investment banking. However, now we turn to the specialist system, which has been fundamental to the Exchange since the late 1800s.

During the early years of the specialists, they served principally as brokers in handling limit orders for other brokers, although they also traded for their own accounts.[11] Subsequently, for the first third of the 1900s, the institution flourished and grew. During this time, dealings for the specialists' own accounts substantially increased relative to broker orders. With this growth, the specialists became among the most prosperous and influential Exchange members, as exemplified by their effectively controlling Exchange governance from 1930 through the 1970s. They came to be viewed as a market-stabilizing force and provider of liquidity, which granted them high esteem by the Exchange and by much of the public, as well. Although such a function holds for inactively traded stocks, it is not the case for actively traded issues. In reality, it has been shown that the specialists' attempts to stabilize markets help create volatility in the prices of securities, to the detriment of the public.[12] This has been known by the SEC since prior to 1940, as evidenced by Douglas (1940), "...the specialists either create the daily price fluctuations or contribute materially to their severity."[13]

Over these four decades, specialists came under increased public scrutiny because of their joint role as broker and dealer. However, also during this time, competition among specialists

---

[11] Oesterle, et al., p. 240. Much of the remainder of this section is adapted from this article.

[12] Professor John Jackson, in Anderson (1992) displays how this increased volatility occurs. Oesterle, et al., show that volatility in the U.K. decreased after jobbers were essentially replaced by a computer trading system.

[13] Douglas, 1940, *Democracy and Finance*, p. 69.

evaporated with no stock being assigned to more than one specialist unit by 1985.[14] In the 1930s some of the more active stocks had been traded by up to six specialists. This increased monopolistic presence of the individual specialist may well have contributed to the specialists' apparent inability to handle the large-block trades that would become prevalent in the 1970s because of increased institutional activity. Evidence of the specialists' inability to handle such activity may be seen in the 1987 and 1989 abrupt market declines, wherein several stocks were halted from trading because of buy-and-sell imbalances. It should also be noted that since the 1970s, there has evolved a substantial amount of listed stocks' being traded away from the specialists.

The above issues, in conjunction with the numerous scandals of the past several years, have led many to call for a revamping of the trading system, and possibly even of the Exchange itself.[15] Probably most widespread is the call for a conversion to an electronic trading system which would replace the trading specialist. However, some, such as Oesterle, et al. (1992), have called for a major revamping of the Exchange itself and have made suggestions for such an implementation:

> Mechanically, the Exchange could restructure through a merger of the existing not-for-profit corporation into a newly-formed for-profit corporation. Exchange members would exchange their membership rights for new common stock in the surviving for-profit corporation . . . The new stock would confer on holders'

---

[14] According to Oesterle, et al, specialists gained an estimated return on an equity of approximately 37% annually from 1980 to 1987, a return much greater than that for the average NYSE member, p. 259.

[15] See Stein, "Looking Beyond the NYSE," (2005), p. 1.

traditional, transferable equity rights to the assets and distributions of the Exchange. [16]

If effected, such developments may render the NYSE specialist to the same fate as that of the jobber in the United Kingdom after the Big Bang in 1986. Thereafter, much of the activity began to be conducted electronically in rooms off the exchange floor. Will such changes come to pass? What is certain is that sweeping changes are in the works, as seen in the following quote from "NYSE to merge with Archipelago: NASDAQ to buy Instinet":

> New York Stock Exchange (NYSE) announced last Wednesday that it has agreed definitively to merge with Chicago-based Archipelago Exchange (ArcaEx) and form a new publicly traded, for-profit company known as NYSE Group... in a "stock for membership" deal, in which NYSE members are to receive cash and 70% of newly issued stock, and Archipelago's shareholders would receive 30% of the new stock"...said John A. Thain, CEO of the NYSE. "As we look to the future and to the challenge of competing globally in a high-speed electronically connected world, it is clear that we must do more. [17]

As seen above, the past decades have witnessed many changes in the environment for investment management relative to commissions and to trading on the Exchange. Available commissions as a direct cost of transactions have declined because of competitive rates. Other competitive forces have resulted in stocks being traded away from the Exchange floor, which often yields better executions for investors. The old system of 1/8 dollar

---

[16] Oesterle, et al., p. 309.

[17] From *Wikinews*, April 24, 2005.

spreads has been replaced by decimal spreads, thus benefiting the public. These past changes, in conjunction with those that appear on the horizon, may work for the advantage of investment managers, especially when viewed in the context of days past. Now we turn to investment banking.

3.3 Investment Banking

The second investment-related entity fundamental in forming the backdrop for today's investment management environment is investment banking, as adeptly depicted by Brandeis (1914).

> The original function of the investment banker was that of dealer in bonds, stocks and notes; buying mainly at wholesale from corporations, municipalities, states and governments which need money, and selling to those seeking investments. The banker performs, in this respect, the function of a merchant; and the function is a very useful one. . . The bonds and stocks of the more important corporations are owned, in large part, by small investors, who do not participate in the management of the company. . . For a small investor to make an intelligent selection from these many corporate securities – indeed, to pass an intelligent judgment upon a single one – is ordinarily impossible . . . he needs the advice of an expert, . . . [18]

According to Krooss and Blyn, it was private banking houses that began as money brokers or "note shavers," who are considered the American forerunners of today's investment bankers. In addition to buying discounted paper, they engaged in: factoring (buying accounts receivable), insuring, lottery selling, and

---

[18] pp. 6-8,

banking, in addition to some stock exchange activity. As a rule, these operations led a precarious life for three reasons: (1) there was little investment banking activity in a developing economy; (2) ties with English investment banking houses were necessary for survival; and (3) their structure as family enterprises made failure almost certain. Also, panics and depressions, and particularly that of 1837, caused many of the pioneer investment houses that had dabbled in securities to fail.[19]

Although the small private banks' role was important in this early arena, it was Nicholas Biddle as President of the Bank of the United States who was the first to act as an investment banker in today's capacity. He participated in: advising, underwriting, refinancing, reorganizing, and protecting the market. After the Bank of the United States lost its federal charter in 1832, Biddle placed greater emphasis on investment banking in the Bank of the United States of Pennsylvania, which came to resemble the European institutions that combined commercial banking with large-scale investment banking. This too closed its doors in 1841.

The investment banking sector had been severely damaged in the late 1830s, but it recovered strongly over the next two decades. This recovery was due largely to the demand for funds which were necessary for large-scale services, such as sewers, water supplies, and early rail projects. Thereafter, the investment banks saw their halcyon days during the last half of the century. This was because of the booming national income, high savings, and increased demand for railroad financing. One of the most famous early promoters of the period was J. Cooke, who participated in a wide variety of financing projects and introduced the method of selling securities widespread rather than to only persons of large fortune. Other familiar names include: Lehman Brothers, Goldman Sachs & Co., J. P. Morgan, and Kidder Peabody, among many of the more prominent investment bankers. As noted by Krooss and

---

[19] Krooss and Blyn, p.34.

Blyn, the investment banking industry was characterized by both entrepreneurship and family connections. Although the large money center participants most quickly come to mind, many of the small country banks throughout the nation also engaged in investment banking alongside their commercial banking activities. Thus was laid the background for the rapid expansion of industry during the period 1890-1929. This era of "financial capitalism" would have been nearly impossible without the assistance of investment bankers who through their influence over investment capital provided the financing for both new and consolidated ventures.

Of great importance, as noted by Krooss and Blyn, "the larger New York City banks entered into alliances with such leading investment banking houses as J. P. Morgan & Co. and Kuhn, Loeb & Co., becoming in effect something of investment banks themselves." Also, foreshadowing future trends:

> In 1908 the First National Bank of New York, already closely affiliated with investment banking, took a gigantic step forward and organized its own investment banking subsidiary, the First Securities Company, as a holding company to acquire shares that the parent company was barred from holding. The National City Bank followed suit three years later by forming the National City Company.[20]

Throughout this period the importance of investment banks was enhanced by their influence with the sources of money on one hand and with corporate demanders of credit on the other. To a great extent, therefore, the flow of credit directly into the securities markets took place under the guidance of the leaders of high finance.

---

[20] Krooss and Blyn, p. 135.

The advent of the 1920s introduced an era of excesses in the investment arena that some financiers welcomed, but others loathed. For one, investment houses turned to underwriting issues for almost any client they could find.

> Conservative investment bankers abhorred the aggressive ways of competition. Otto Kahn of Kuhn, Loeb & Co. later recalled with a shudder "the kind of competition which we had between 1926 and 1929, when, to my knowledge fifteen American bankers sat in Belgrade, Jugoslavia, making bids, and a dozen American bankers sat in half a dozen South and Central American States, or in the Balkan States . . . one outbidding the other, foolishly, recklessly. . . ."[21]

Also, it was necessary that the banking and brokerage houses would have to unload these securities on the public. However, this was not difficult owing to the public psychology which Otto Kahn summed up nicely: "The public . . . were determined that every piece of paper should be worth tomorrow twice what it was today." In the frenzy to sell securities, it was inevitable that some houses would employ questionable and sometimes even fraudulent selling tactics. For even though the public was eager to buy securities, the brokerage houses and security affiliates of banks urged public trading to generate even faster turnovers. For example, the National City Co. ran "sales contests" in which prizes were awarded to salesmen with the most securities sold. Ivy-league graduates were recruited en masse and, after a brief training period, were turned loose on the investing public. As one of these brokers stated, "What counted for us was the business of keeping our customers trading in and out of securities, so that win or lose we

---

[21] Ibid., p.163.

gathered our brokers fees at fifteen dollars for each hundred shares." [22]

The ensuing market collapse and revelations about the shenanigans of Wall Street led to a public outrage against the investments industry. The new administration in Washington shared the public's disenchantment with Wall Street, and President Roosevelt announced that the "practices of the unscrupulous money changers stand indicted in the court of public opinion, rejected by the hearts and minds of men . . . The money changers have fled from their high seats in the temple of our civilization. We may now restore that temple to the ancient truths."[23]

Over the following months the New Deal attempted to substantially remake the environment in which Wall Street carried on business. Among the responses was the Banking Act of 1933, which barred any financial institution from simultaneously engaging in investment banking operations and in commercial banking operations.

In addition to the impact of legislation, the economic environment of the 1930s dealt the investment banking industry a devastating blow. The volume of security issues nose-dived from approximately $11.6 billion in 1929 to $1.1 billion in 1933. This decline, combined with a huge contraction in stock exchange activity, had a crushing effect on the industry, especially on those investment bankers with large sales organizations. The 1930s also saw the rise of private placements, which would diminish sharply the business of investment bankers. Because of legislation, declining volumes, and changes within the industry, investment banks never fully recovered in the post-Depression decades, as did other financial intermediaries.

---

[22] Ibid., p.165.

[23] Ibid., p. 194.

It was not until the late 1950s that the dollar volume of sales on the Exchange again matched the 1926 level of sales, and it was not until 1967 that trading surpassed the record set in 1929. However, underwriting activities did not recover to the same degree for various reasons. Compared with earlier periods, business firms financed a greater proportion of their needs via internal financing: retained earnings and depreciation allowances. Secondly, new aggressive financial intermediaries enabled business firms to bypass the investment bankers and the new issues market through mortgages, term loans, short-term financing, and leasing. Thirdly, private placements, mostly with life insurance companies and corporate pension plans, which had played a modest role in the1930s, assumed more importance in the '50s and '60s, as seen in a majority of new corporate bond issues being privately placed in the early 1960s.

Although the investment banking industry experienced substantial competition from new types of intermediaries over the last three decades of the 20th century, the industry experienced an enormous increase in the dollar volume of securities transactions. There was considerable consolidation in the industry, as some of the old-line brokerage houses merged with other houses which had large retail sales forces. During this period the discount commission sector made substantial in-roads into the full-service brokerage market. It is appropriate to note here that commissions at the inception of the Exchange and during the first decades of the 1900s, as noted above, approximated ¼% to ½%, in sharp contrast to the approximately 2% for a transaction around 1975.

However, massive television and other media promotion were undertaken in an attempt to protect the high-commission business vestiges of pre-1975 days. Increased emphasis was placed on the retailing of high-commission mutual funds (as seen in the next section), and managed money accounts became widely promoted. During the last decade of the 1900s, the underwriting business boomed with the public offerings of internet stocks. It was at this time that the Glass-Steagel Act was repealed.

The ramifications of this change may ultimately be huge for the investment management environment. Under this new regime, financial institutions such as investment banks, insurance companies, credit card companies, and others, are allowed to merge and thereby create mega-financial institutions. Many mergers have already occurred, and it will be a matter of time before it can be determined whether these mega-financial institutions will be a benefit to investors, especially investors at the individual level. Now we turn to the third of our investment-related entities of interest: the investment companies.

3.4 Investment Companies

The third of the investment-related entities which strongly impacted the backdrop for today's investment management environment are investment companies. The most popular type of investment company in the United States today is the mutual fund which adopted its present open-end structure in the 1920s, more than a century after the earliest investment companies originated. Some consider the first investment company to be *Societé Général de Belgique*, which was established by King William I of Belgium in the early 1800s.[24] Similar trusts were also formed by Swiss bankers to separate investment properties from commercial banking operations, but these trusts did not become popular as investment vehicles until they blossomed in England and Scotland during the period 1863-87. Others trace the origins of investment companies in the United States to the Massachusetts Hospital Life

---

[24] The first three pages of this section are primarily adapted from Anderson and Born, 1992, *Closed-End Investment Companies: Issues and Answers*, pp.7-12, and from Kroos and Blyn, pp. 199-203.

Insurance Company, which in 1823 first accepted and pooled funds on behalf of contributors for a fee of ½ of 1%. Yet, some refer to the New York Stock Trust (1889) or to the Boston Personal Property Trust (1893), which was the first company organized to offer small investors a diversified portfolio as an investment company.

Regardless of the precise origin, the growth of American investment companies was gradual from 1889 to 1924, during which time 18 investment companies were formed in the United States. These companies had varied purposes, ranging from a near-holding company (Railway and Light Securities Company) to an essentially modern closed-end investment company (Boston Personal Property Trust).

However, American investment trusts grew in earnest during the economic boom of the 1920s. As wealth increased, the general public became interested in the stock market, and a number of trusts catered to these investors. Most of these closed-end funds were patterned after British companies which invested primarily for stable growth, income, and diversification. However, of greater importance to the future of the industry was the emergence in 1924 of the first open-end fund, Massachusetts Investors Trust. This fund, the first of the modern mutual funds, allowed shareholders to redeem their shares at net asset value, less $2 per share.

As the 1920s roared on, eager investors regarded many of the earlier trusts as too conservative, and newer companies were formed to appeal to these more adventurous investors. The popularity of speculative funds exploded. In 1923, there were 15 investment companies with total capital of approximately $15 million; by 1929, the industry's approximately 675 funds had total capital close to $7 billion. Most of the new funds used some form of leverage in their capital structure. On average, 40% of their capital consisted of bonds and preferred equity.

Many of these speculative investment companies ignored safety and income considerations, focusing instead on share price appreciation. When the market crashed, many investors lost vast sums in these shares. According to a later Securities and Exchange Commission report, by the end of 1937, the average dollar invested in 1929 in the index of leveraged closed-end fund stocks was worth 5¢, while a non-leveraged dollar was worth 48¢.

After the abuses of investment companies during the 1920s and the tremendous losses suffered in the stock market crash of 1929, investors began to seek security in their investments. The redemption policies of open-end investment companies offered more security than closed-end investment companies, and the open-end companies gained popularity, while the number of closed-end funds diminished.

Believing that both the investment and banking businesses had performed poorly during the Panic, many investors and politicians called for investigations and regulation. The first major piece of legislation, the Securities Act of 1933, set basic requirements for virtually all companies that sell securities. Briefly, the act requires that publicly traded companies furnish shareholders with full and accurate financial and corporate information. Although the act went a long way toward regulating new security offerings, it did not apply to outstanding securities. The Securities Exchange Act of 1934 formed the Securities and Exchange Commission and gave it broad powers over the industry, such as the ability to impose minimum accounting and financial standards on interstate brokers and dealers.

However, it was the Investment Company Act of 1940 that covered the formation, management, and public offerings of every investment company that has more than 50 security holders or that proposes to offer securities to the public. The Act of 1940 ended the unrestrained and often unethical practices by which investment companies had been formed, floated, and operated in the United States.

Since the passage of the Act of 1940, mutual funds have proliferated, and today are the dominant vehicles for channeling the savings of U.S. investors into financial assets. In recent years, assets under management by these organizations are estimated to be $7 trillion managed by approximately 7000 funds, as seen in Figure 3.1. Over the past decade alone, the number of funds has increased more than three-fold. During the growth of this industry, there has been considerable change which has significantly impacted the environment for today's investment manager, as we shall now see.

Figure 3.1: Growth of Mutual Funds in the U.S.

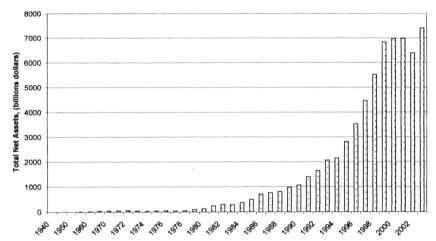

Over the first 30 years of modern mutual funds, they were generally sold to the public with a sales charge up to 8.5%, which declined with quantity purchases. However, industry competition in the 1970s brought about no-load funds, which appealed to many investors. Thereafter, the industry introduced rear-load and level-load funds for competitive purposes. Public redemptions of funds' shares during the late 1970s further exacerbated declining industry profit margins.   In response, the industry campaigned for and succeeded in the charging of 12b-1 fees under the guise of compensating brokers for discouraging clients' share redemptions.

These and other changes have ultimately impacted investor returns in conflicting ways, and the net effect is not readily obvious.   However, some recent insights into these industry matters have been made by a prominent leader in mutual funds. For these insights we turn to some of the points made in "The Mutual Fund Industry 60 Years Later: For Better or Worse?" by John C. Bogle, founder of the Vanguard Group.   According to Bogle, in addition to the increase in the size of the industry:

> It has also undergone a multi-faceted change in character. In 1945, it was an industry engaged primarily in the profession of serving investors and striving to meet the standards of the recently enacted Investment Company Act of 1940, which established the policy that funds must be "organized, operated, and managed" in the interests of their shareholders *rather than* in the interests of their managers and distributors.   It was an industry that focused primarily on stewardship. Today, in contrast, the industry is a vast and highly successful marketing business, an industry focused primarily on salesmanship. [25]

Bogle reviews numerous changes that have occurred over the last six decades. He explains that funds have become larger, more numerous, and more heterogeneous in their objectives.   Also, individual portfolio managers now manage funds rather than committees, as in the past. Today, funds trade much more actively

---

[25] *Financial Analysts Journal*, Jan./Feb., 2005, pp. 15-24.

than previously, with portfolio turnover rates often exceeding 100% annually, compared to 25% or less in earlier times. Investors in funds also trade their funds more than twice as often, and on average hold a fund only four years. In addition, the cost of fund ownership, as measured by the average expense ratio, has doubled from 0.76% to 1.56% annually.

The issues of expenses and of portfolio turnover are of particular importance to the investment manager today. When the impact of expenses and turnover are considered, the combined annual cost to fund shareholders is approximately 2.5% today, compared to 1.7% six decades earlier. According to Bogle, the impact of these combined expenses results in the average fund today delivering only 79% of the market's annual return, compared to 89% of the market's return over the 1945-1965 period.

3.5 Summary

Over the past two centuries the stock exchange, investment banking, and investment companies, have evolved in close conjunction with each other in shaping today's financial arena. The stock exchange has often been viewed by many as being little more than a gambling establishment. Nevertheless, it is via security pricing that much of our economic capital is ultimately allocated to productive assets. However, to protect the economic position of the members of the Exchange, excess rents in the form of fixed commissions and specialists' frictions have long been a part of the market environment. Vestiges of these factors, albeit to a lesser degree, remain as forces to be reckoned with by today's investment managers.

The second investment-related entity of interest considered above, is investment banking. This industry, which has been fundamental to our economic process via underwriting and related activities, is also the interface between investment managers and the stock exchanges through its brokerage operations. In recent decades the industry has aggressively marketed mutual funds, annuities, and other high-fee products aimed primarily at individual investors. These financial institutions are a dominant force in the investment landscape with which investment managers have to contend.

As to the third of the investment-related entities of interest, today's mutual funds offer both opportunities and potential pitfalls in the plethora of products available and their varied fee structures. This complex maze of choices will continue to challenge both professional and individual managers. Now that we have briefly reviewed the historical backdrop for today's investment manager, the following chapters address many of the research findings to date relative to both today's investment environment and to managers' activities in this environment.

IV: MARKET EFFICIENCY AND ANOMALIES

4.1 Introduction

In this chapter we present findings from several of the more frequently cited academic articles dealing with the issues both of market efficiency and of anomalies. This treatment is not exhaustive, but is intended to present an overview of these issues relative to the investment environment in which portfolio managers operate.

4.2 Two Schools of Thought

Over the past decades two basic schools of thought have evolved concerning the usefulness of public information in the investment process. One group, the "efficient markets" theorists, claims that security prices fully reflect all available information. In such a context the practical implication is that investors will not benefit by using publicly available information. A wide variety of studies addressing both individual security investing and mutual fund investing (the topic of Chapter 5), including that of Malkiel (1995), lend credence to this view, which for many has come to be the acceptable view in the investments arena.

The more traditional school of thought contends that informed traders can earn a return on their activity of information-gathering by using their costly information to take positions in the market which are "better" than the positions of uninformed traders (see

Grossman and Stiglitz, 1980).[26]   The essence of this position is
elucidated in the works of Grossman (1975, 1976, 1978) and of
Kihlstrom and Mirman (1975), among others.   Rather than
paraphrasing these works, we defer to Grossman and Stiglitz's
contribution to this issue, as presented in "On the Impossibility of
Informationally Efficient Markets."

The following excerpts clearly describe their position:

> If competitive equilibrium is defined as a situation in
> which prices are such that all arbitrage profits are
> eliminated, is it possible that a competitive economy
> always be in equilibrium? Clearly not, for then those
> who arbitrage make no (private) return from their
> (privately) costly activity. Hence the assumptions that all
> markets, including that for information, are always in
> equilibrium   and   always   perfectly   arbitraged   are
> inconsistent when arbitrage is costly.

> We   propose   here   a   model   in   which   there   is   an
> equilibrium degree of disequilibrium: prices reflect the
> information of informed individuals (arbitrageurs) but
> only partially, so that those who expend resources to
> obtain   information   do   receive   compensation.   How
> informative the price system is depends on the number
> of individuals who are informed; but the number of
> individuals who are informed is itself an endogenous
> variable in the model.

> The model is the simplest one in which prices perform a
> well-articulated role in conveying information from the
> informed to the uninformed. When informed individuals
> observe information that the return to a security is going
> to be high, they bid its price up, and conversely when

---

[26] It is obvious from early works such as that of Schabacker (1930) that many
investors have traditionally held a similar view of the value of information.

they observe information that the return is going to be low. Thus the price system makes publicly available the information obtained by informed individuals to the uninformed. In general, however, it does this imperfectly; this is perhaps lucky, for were it to do it perfectly, an equilibrium would not exist.[27]

In their concluding remarks the authors state, "We have argued that because information is costly, prices cannot perfectly reflect the information which is available, since if it did, those who spent resources to obtain it would receive no compensation."

4.3 Challenges to the Efficient Markets View

Although many in both the professional investments arena and in academics hold that the efficient markets view best describes the investments world, there has evolved a substantial body of empirical research that seriously challenges this position. These numerous works date from the 1980s and continue apace. For purposes of expediency we quote the article of Daniel, Hirshleifer, and Subrahmanyam (1998), who categorize the various works and their findings. These findings are often termed "anomalous" owing to their inconsistencies with the efficient markets view of investments. The following quotation is presented by Daniel, et al. in their article. Their detailed "Appendix A" is included at the end of this chapter.

> In recent years a body of evidence on security returns has presented a sharp challenge to the traditional view [here the author uses the term "traditional" to refer to the efficient markets view which has its origins in the mid-

---

[27] p. 393.

1900s] that securities are rationally priced to reflect all publicly available information. Some of the more pervasive anomalies can be classified as follows:

1. Event-based return predictability (public-event-date average stock returns of the same sign as average subsequent long-run abnormal performance)
2. Short-term momentum (positive short-term autocorrelation of stock returns, for individual stocks and the market as a whole)
3. Long-term reversal (negative autocorrelation of short-term returns separated by long lags, or "overreaction")
4. High volatility of assets prices relative to fundamentals
5. Short-run post-earnings announcement stock price "drift" in the direction indicated by the earnings surprise, but abnormal stock price performance in the opposite direction of long-term earnings changes.

There remains disagreement over the interpretation of the above evidence of predictability. One possibility is that these anomalies are chance deviations to be expected under market efficiency (Fama, 1998). We believe the evidence does not accord with this viewpoint because some of the return patterns are strong and regular. The size, book-to-market, and momentum effects are present both internationally and in different time periods. Also, the pattern mentioned in (1.) above obtains for the great majority of event studies.

Alternatively, these patterns could represent variations in rational risk premia. However, based on the high Sharpe ratios (relative to the market) apparently achievable with simple trading strategies (MacKinlay, 1995), any assert pricing model consistent with these patterns would have to have extremely variable marginal utility across states. Campbell and Cochrane (1994) find that a utility function with extreme habit persistence is required to explain the predictable variation in market returns. To be consistent with cross-sectional predictability findings (e.g., on size, book-to-market, and momentum), a model would presumably require even more extreme variation in marginal utilities. Also, the model would require that marginal utilities covary strongly with the returns on the size, book-to-market, and momentum portfolios. But when the data are examined, no such correlation is obvious. Given this evidence, it seems reasonable to consider explanations for the observed return patterns based on imperfect rationality.[28]

4.4 Summary

To summarize, there exist two opposing schools of thought concerning the usefulness of public information in the investment process: (1) the "efficient markets" theorists who claim that investors cannot benefit by using public information, and (2) the more traditional school which contents that investors who expend resources to obtain information can receive compensation for their efforts. Now that we have briefly reviewed the two opposing schools of thought, we turn our attention to one of the primary sources of information used widely by both individuals and professional portfolio managers: analysts' recommendations. Is this public information of value in the investments process?

---

[28] pp. 1839-1840.

APPENDIX 4A:
SECURITIES PRICE PATTERNS

This appendix cites the relevant literature for the anomalies mentioned in the first paragraph quoted from Daniel, et al. above. According to the authors, out-of-sample tests (in time and location) have established several of these patterns as regularities.

Underreaction to Public News Events (event-date average stock returns of the same sign as average subsequent long-run abnormal performance)

1. Stock splits (Grinblatt, Masulis, and Titman (1984). Desai and Jain (1997), and Ikenberry, Rankine, and Stice (1996))
2. Tender offer and open market repurchases (Lakonishok and Vermaelen (1990), Ikenberry, Lakonishok, and Vermaelen (1995))
3. Analyst recommendations (Groth et al. (1979), Bjerring, Lakonishok, and Vermaelen (1983), Elton et al. (1984), Womack (1996). And Michaely and Womack (1999)),
4. Dividend initiations and omissions (Michaely, Thaler, and Womack (1995))
5. Seasoned issues of common stock (Loughran and Ritter (1995), Spiess and Affleck-Graves (1995), Teoh, Welch, and Wong 1998), but see the differing evidence for Japan of Kang, Kim, and Stulz (1996)
6. Earnings surprises (at least for a period after the event) (Bernard and Thomas 1989, 1990), Brown and Pope (1996))
7. Public announcement of previous insider trades (Seyhun (1997); see also Seyhun (1986, 1988) and Rozeff and Zaman (1988))

8. Venture capital share distributions (Gompers and Lerner (1998)).

There is also evidence that earnings forecasts underreact to public news, such as quarterly earnings announcements (Abarbanell (1991), Abarbanell and Bernard (1992), Medenhall (1991). An event inconsistent with this generalization is exchange listing (McConnel and Sanger (1987), Dharan and Ikenberry (1995)). Fama (1998) argues that some of these anomalous return patterns are sensitive to empirical methodology. On the other hand, Loughran and Ritter (1997) argue that the methodology favored by Fama minimizes the power to detect possible misevaluation effects.

Short-Term Momentum (positive short-term autocorrelation of stock returns, for individual stocks and the market as a whole)

See Jegadeesh and Titman (1993) and Daniel (1996). "Short" here refers to periods on the order of six to twelve months. At very short horizons there is negative autocorrelation in individual stock returns (Jegadeesh (1990), Lehmann (1990)), probably resulting from bid-ask spreads and other measurement problems (Kaul and Nimalendran (1990)). Rouwenhorst (1998a) finds evidence of momentum in twelve European countries. The effect is stronger for smaller firms. However, Haugen and Baker (1996) and Daniel (1996) show that, although there is evidence of a strong book-to-market effect in Japan, there is little or no evidence of a momentum effect. Rouwenhorst (1998a) reports a strong momentum effect within and across twelve European countries, and Rouwenhorst (1998b) finds evidence that momentum, firm size, and value predict common stock returns in twenty emerging markets.

Long-term Reversal (negative autocorrelation of short-term returns separated by long lags, or "overreaction")

Cross-sectionally, see DeBondt and Thaler (1985, 1987), and Chopra, Lakonishok, and Ritter (1992); on robustness issues, see Fama and French (1996) and Ball, Kothari, and Shanken (1995). For the aggregate market, see Fama and French (1988) and Poterba and Summers (1988); internationally, see Richards (1997). On the robustness of the finding in the post-WWII period, see Kim, Nelson, and Startz (1988), Carmel and Young (1997), Asness (1995), and Daniel (1996); the latter two papers show that in post-WWII U.S. data, significant cross-sectional (Asness) and aggregate (Daniel) long-horizon negative autocorrelations are partly masked by a momentum effect (positive serial correlation) at approximately a one-year horizon.

Unconditional Excess Volatility of Asset Prices Relative to Fundamentals

See Shiller (1981, 1989); for critical assessments of this conclusion, see Kleidon (1986) and Marsh and Merton (1986).

Abnormal Stock Price Performance in the Opposite Direction of Long-Term Earnings Changes

DeBondt and Thaler (1987), and Lakonishok, Shleifer, and Vishny (1994) find a negative relation between long-horizon returns and past financial performance measures such as earnings or sales growth; see however Dechow and Sloan (1997). This implies that one or more short-horizon, long-lag regression coefficients must be negative (proof available on request). In contrast, Chan, Jegadeesh, and Lakonishok (1996) do not reject the null of no such a negative relation, perhaps owing to a lack of power in detecting long-run reversals. Also, La Porta et al. (1997) find large positive returns for value stocks on earnings announcements dates (and negative growth stocks).

In addition to the anomalies studies above, there are also the works related to earning surprises such as that by Latané and Jones (1977), Joy, Litzenberger and McEnally (1977), and Jones, Rendleman and Latané (1985), among others. Most of these studies indicate that standardized unexpected earnings (SUE) have a significant impact on security excess returns, with most of the impact occurring after the announcement date. In a different vein, there is evidence that closed-end investment companies' (CEICs) shares may often be priced relative to net asset value so as to allow profitable trading strategies over time. Over the past two decades, studies addressing this issue include those of Richards, Frazer, and Groth (1980), Anderson (1986, 1989), Anderson, et al. (2001), and Sias (1997).

V: THE EFFICACY OF ANALYSTS' RECOMMENDATIONS

5.1 Introduction

As seen in the prior chapter, numerous studies of investment anomalies appear in the academic literature. One area of interest that is particularly germane to this book is that of analysts' recommendations, a topic addressed in multiple studies over the past decades. Among the questions asked are: (1) Are analysts correct in predicting winners and losers? (2) Can investors profit from analysts' recommendations? (3) How do prices adjust to recommendations? and (4) Are analysts honest in their recommendations?

Because analysts' recommendations are likely the most readily available public information accessible to both individual and professional portfolio managers, this chapter summarizes in varying degrees several representative works pertaining to the above questions. The sources of advice include, *Value Line* and *Morningstar*, professional research organizations such as *Standard and Poor's*, popular outlets such as *Forbes* and the *Wall Street Journal*, brokerage house research departments, and others. We now turn to several studies which investigate the efficacy of and impact of this type of information. [29]

5.2 "Can Stock Market Forecasters Forecast?"

The earliest study of which we are aware that pertains to the effectiveness of investment advice is "Can Stock Market

---

[29] This overview of the literature is representative, but not exhaustive.

Forecasters Forecast?" by Alfred Cowles 3rd, which appeared in 1933. The findings of this work are prescient of the efficient markets view of investment returns, which would become widely popular decades thereafter. The initial section of the work addresses the stock selection success of 20 fire insurance companies and 16 financial services. The second part deals with the stock market forecasting skills of 25 financial publications.

The first series of tests include the evaluation of 7,500 separate recommendations made by 16 leading financial services over the 4½ years ending July, 1932. Step one is the recording of each stock recommendation for each week, and this is followed by the tabulation of all off-setting transactions. With this information, the gain or loss is calculated for each round trip transaction and compared to the gain or loss of the overall market for the same period. Funds are equally redistributed among all stocks at the beginning of every six-month period. Compounding the six-month records yields the percentage by which each service's recommendations exceeds or falls behind the overall market. It is seen that the average annual rate of return is – 1.43% relative to the bogey.

In Cowles' investigation of the common stock investments of 20 leading fire insurance companies, the author explains that these companies have a lengthy history of investing compared to both financial services and to investment companies, which are of relatively recent origin. Because the insurance companies' average portfolio turnover is only about 5% a year, the analysis is confined to the actual purchases and sales during the examination period rather than to the entire stock portfolio. The methodology employed, however, is essentially the same as with the investments services. It is seen that the stocks selected for investment effectively underperform the stock market by approximately 1.20% annually.

In Cowles' second series of tests, he first considers the market forecasting record of William Peter Hamilton, who employed the Dow Theory for forecasting purposes. (For a discussion of Dow Theory, see Cowles, p. 315.) As editor of the *Wall Street Journal*, Hamilton wrote 255 editorials over 26 years, which presented stock market forecasts. Based on these editorials, Hamilton was a buyer of stocks, seller of stocks, and out of the market, 55%, 16%, and 29% of the time, respectively. For the period 1903 through 1929, Hamilton would have earned a return of 12% annually, compared to the overall market return of 15.5% annually, as a control.

In the final set of tests, more than 3,300 forecasts are compiled from 24 financial publications from January 1, 1928, to June 1, 1932. The question is asked, "In the light of what this particular bulletin says, would one be led to buy stocks with all the funds at his disposal, or place a portion only of his funds in stocks, or withdraw entirely from the market?" On the basis of this, the funds are allocated to the market in proportions ranging from zero to 100%.

Using an involved scoring system, the author reports that only one-third of the list of forecasts was successful. Thus, he concludes that the average forecast earned approximately 4% per annum below what would have been earned randomly. After further discussion of the statistical interpretation of the results found, the author concludes the article with the following summary:

> 1. Sixteen financial services, in making some 7500 recommendations of individual common stocks for investment during the period from January 1, 1928, to July 1, 1932, compiled an average record that was worse than that of the average common stock by 1.43 per cent annually. Statistical tests of the best individual records failed to demonstrate that they exhibited skill, and

indicated that they more probably were the results of chance.

2. Twenty fire insurance companies in making a similar selection of securities during the years 1928 to 1931, inclusive, achieved an average record 1.20 per cent annually worse than that of the general run of stocks. The best of these records, since it is not very much more impressive than the record of the most successful of the sixteen financial services, fails to exhibit definitely the existence of any skill in investment.

3. William Peter Hamilton, editor of the *Wall Street Journal*, publishing forecasts of the stock market based on the Dow Theory over a period of 26 years, from 1904 to 1929, inclusive, achieved a result better than what would ordinarily be regarded as a normal investment return, but poorer than the result of a continuous outright investment in representative common stocks for this period. On 90 occasions he announced changes in the outlook for the market. Forty-five of these predictions were successful, and 45 unsuccessful.

4. Twenty-four financial publications engaged in forecasting the stock market during the 4 1/2 years from January 1, 1928, to June 1, 1932, failed as a group by 4 per cent per annum to achieve a result as good as the average of all purely random performances. A review of the various statistical tests, applied to the records for this period, of these 24 forecasters, indicates that the most successful records are little, if any, better than what might be expected to result from pure chance. There is some evidence, on the other hand, to indicate that the

least successful records are worse than what could reasonably be attributed to chance.[30]

We have summarized Cowles' work in much greater detail than will be done with those works that follow. The reasons for this are: (1) As the first of this type of investigation, the article is truly path-breaking and comprehensive. (2) The breadth of the investigation involves stock investing by insurance companies and recommendations by financial services, as well as overall market forecasting; and (3) The sheer magnitude of this study, which was done manually, is unique. Next, we briefly address several of the more recent studies in this arena.

5.3 More Recent Evidence

Following Cowles, decades passed before the publication of more studies dealing with analysts' recommendations. Some of the earlier studies address the formulation of investment strategies based on *Value Line*'s timeliness rankings, which attempt to measure probable stock price performance over the next six to twelve months.

Studies by Black (1973) and by Copeland and Mayers (1982) examine whether excess returns can be earned by buying stocks in *Value Line*'s top rank (ranking 1) and shorting stocks in the lowest rank (ranking 5). Black, using monthly portfolio rebalancing and a capital asset pricing model technique, reports a 20% annual excess return before transactions expense. In a slightly different vein, Copeland and Mayers use a standard market model with semi-annual portfolio rebalancing and report annual excess returns of 6.8% before transactions costs. Holloway (1981) examines top-ranking stocks with both a buy-and-hold strategy (a one-year

---

[30] p. 323.

horizon) and an active strategy (weekly rebalancing) and reports excess returns before transactions costs for both strategies. However, when transactions costs are considered, the active strategies' excess returns are eliminated, but the buy-and-hold strategy produces 8.6% annually.

Also, during this time, studies begin to appear that examine abnormal returns around the occurrence of analysts' recommendations. As is seen in Table 5.1 on the next page, these studies involve announcements which usually appear in major news publications. Column 4 in this table illustrates the abnormal returns at announcement and their t-statistics (in parenthesis), with most studies reporting significant abnormal returns of the anticipated sign. Column 5 shows equivalents for the post-announcement period, along with the length of the period of interest in square brackets.

Many of these event studies find significant abnormal returns around the announcement of analysts' recommendations, and a reversal in the securities' prices in the days that follow. Among the studies listed in the table, Groth, et al. (1979) report that a significant number of stocks experience larger returns prior to the announcement of a positive recommendation than afterward. Bjerring, et al. (1983) report a gradual reflection over time of the valuable information contained in recommendations. Both Liu, et al. (1990) and Davies and Canes (1978) report that prices adjust to analysts' recommendations too quickly for profitable exploitation of this information. The authors of the study from which we adapted Table 5.1 are Barber and Loeffler (1993), who examine the impact of analysts' recommendations appearing in the "Dartboard" column in the *Wall Street Journal*. To test the impact of these recommendations, the authors compare the featured stocks' returns to the returns of the randomly chosen "Dartboard" stocks. Overall, they find significant price return of over 4% for the featured stocks versus no price impact for the control group.

Table 5.1: Review of Second-Hand Information Literature.

Researcher	Type of Recommendation	Period	Abn. Ret (%) Anmt.	Abn. Ret (%) Post-Anmt.
Barber and Loeffler (1993)	Wall Street Journal "Dartboard" Column	1988-90	3.53 (12.19)	-2.08 (-1.56) [2.25]
Liu, Smith, and Syed (1990)	Wall Street Journal "Heard on the Street" Column, Buy Recommendations	1982-85	1.54 (16.37)	-0.94 (-1.67) [2.10]
Liu, Smith, and Syed (1990)	"Heard on the Street" Column, Sell Recommendations	1982-85	-1.99 (-15.46)	-0.32 (-0.37) [2.10]
Pari (1987)	Wall Street Week Guest Recommendations	1983-84	0.66 (5.55)	-1.42 -- [2.9]
Lee (1986)	Heinz Biel's Forbes Recommendations	1962-79	0.87 (1.47)	n.a.
Glascock, Henderson, and Martin (1986)	E.F. Hulton's Aggressive Purchase Recommendations	1982	1.20 (3.10)	12.20 (2.14) [1.90]
Stickel (1985)	Value Line Rank Changes from Rank 2 To Rank 1	1976-80	0.86 (10.92)	0.01 (0.74) [7.50]
Davies and Canes (1978)	Wall Street Journal "Heard on the Street" Column, Buy Recommendations	1970-71	0.92 (9.55)	0.03 -- [2.20]
Davies and Canes (1978)	Wall Street Journal "Heard on the Street" Column, Buy Recommendations	1970-71	-2.37 (-9.87)	0.85 -- [2.20]
Bjerring, Lakonishok, and Vermaelen (1983)	Canadian Brokerage House Recommendations (weekly data)	1977-81	1.49 (3.76)	8.68 (2.90) [1.38]
Groth, Lewellen, Schlarbaum, and Lease (1979)	Brokerage House Recommendations (monthly data)	1964-70	1.56 --	-0.93 -- [1.12]

Reported t-statistics are in parentheses when available. The announcement returns are calculated on the day of the announcement ($t = 0$). The post-announcement returns are calculated over the period in square brackets.

They also report that after approximately one month some of the abnormal return dissolves, but that a portion still exists. The featured stocks outperform the Dow 53% of the time. The authors conclude that there is some value in analysts' recommendations, but it is not clear whether it can be profitably exploited after transactions costs.

Over the same decade, there appear several other types of related studies. For example, Dimson and Marsh (1984) via a UK investment manager collect over 4,000 one-year forecasts on approximately 200 stocks made by 35 entities over the 1980-1981 period. After examining this ex-post data, the authors report a high correlation between forecasted returns and actual returns, which suggests that analysts distinguish winners from losers. However, a substantial part of the information content appears to be discounted in the marketplace during the first month. Nevertheless, an analysis of the forecasts shows that the apparent predictive ability of the recommendations could be translated into superior performance by the fund's investment managers.

In another study Elton, Gruber, and Grossman (1986) use a monthly technique when focusing on a stock's change from a lower to higher rank (upgrades) or vice versa. They report significant beta-adjusted excess returns of 3.4% in the first three months after an upgrade and 2.3% negative returns after a downgrade. They also report that analysts' recommendations are superior to time-series models.

Later, in a 1996 work, Womack investigates a sample of 1573 recommendation changes on 833 stocks by the 14 highest-ranking U.S. brokerage research departments over the period 1989-1991. The author looks at only those recommendations that impact the most attractive category or least attractive category of stocks. It is seen that the ratio of buy-to-sell recommendations is about 7 to 1. The basic findings are that a stock price rises by roughly 3% in the three-day window around a "buy recommendation" and falls by

4.7% in the three-day window on a "sell recommendation." It is also reported that a stock over time tends to move in the direction of the change in recommendation. There is an upward drift of 2.4% in the price of a buy recommendation stock in the first month, compared to a -9.1% drift in a sell recommendation issue over the following 6-month period. In concluding, Womack states:

> The results are consistent with the expanded view of market efficiency suggested by Grossman and Stiglitz (1980): that there must be returns to information search costs. These information search costs are often assumed to be zero when considering the efficient market hypothesis. The nontrivial magnitude of the returns reported here challenges the innocence of that assumption.[31]

The following year, in "An Analysis of *Value Line*'s Ability to Forecast Long-Run Returns," Benesh and Perfect (1997) focus on the accuracy of *Value Line*'s long-run price projections. This study contrasts with earlier studies of Black (1973), Copeland and Mayers (1982), and Holloway (1981), which address the efficacy of *Value Line*'s timeliness ratings involving probable performance over the next six to twelve months. Benesh and Perfect explain that *Value Line*'s mathematical model, which is used to make three- to five-year stock price projections, is based on the stock's current earnings rank, current price rank, and estimated future earnings rank. This last variable is the most critical input to the long-term price projection model.

In their analysis the authors employ data on approximately 1,400 stocks for the fourth quarters of 1982 and 1988, which allow an examination of two non-overlapping five-year periods. They observe that *Value Line*'s long-run return forecasts tend to be

---

[31] p. 166

optimistic. To assess *Value Line*'s ability to forecast long-run returns, they employ two OLS regression techniques. Their findings suggest that *Value Line*'s long-run forecasts are of little use to investors during the periods of analysis, as any significant relationship between actual returns and forecasts is inverse. However, the worth of these forecasts is increased when stocks with a timeliness rating of one are considered.

More recently, in "Can Investors Profit from the Prophets? Security Analysts' Recommendations and Stock Returns," Barber, et al. (2001) investigate whether changes in the consensus rating of stocks provides sufficient returns to offset the transactions costs necessary for capturing these returns. The authors use data for the 1986-1996 period. After considering momentum and Fama-French factors, the authors report that the most highly recommended stocks earn a positive market-adjusted annual return of nearly 4%; while the least favorably recommended stocks earn a negative return of nearly 9%. When they examine daily rebalancing of the buy-and-sell portfolios, turnover exceeds 400% annually, but less frequent rebalancing appears to lower excess returns. However, these returns are very time-sensitive, as when investors act after two weeks, the excess returns are not significantly different from zero. Their findings support earlier studies reporting that the market responds to analysts' information, but this information's value decays quickly over the first one to two months. They conclude that the question of using analysts' recommendations to outperform benchmarks is still an open one.

In a similar work Barber, et al. (2003) essentially repeat the above analysis with a sample of 160,000 real-time recommendations from 299 brokerage houses addressing 9,621 firms for the period 1996-2000. Although their findings for the 1996-1999 period are consistent with their earlier findings, the year 2000 apparently was catastrophic for analysts. That year the least favorably recommended stocks earned an annualized market-adjusted return of over 48%, while the most highly-recommended stocks fell over 31%. This held for most months of the year and was observed for both high-tech and non-tech stocks. They conclude that researchers must be diligent in their analyses because the exclusion of the year 2000 could significantly impact their findings about analysts' stock recommendations.

5.4 Summary

The earliest work investigating the efficacy of analysts' recommendations is that of Cowles (1933). The author reports that recommendations over the 1928-1932 period yield lower returns than the overall market. However, more recent findings show a positive association between *Value Line* timeliness rankings and excess returns. Other studies that focus on buy (sell) recommendations appearing in the media report positive (negative) returns at announcement and over the post-announcement period, albeit it to a lesser degree. Some studies conclude that these returns are attainable after transactions costs, but such findings are not unanimous.

One unusual result reported by Barber et al. (2002) is the finding that returns to favorably recommended stocks over the year 2000 are substantially lower than the returns characterizing the least favorably recommended stocks. It may be speculated that a similar situation to such an unusual occurrence in the depth of the late 1920s bear market could possibly have impacted Cowles' earlier results, as the period of his consideration includes the period following 1929. Regardless, most of these later studies generally show that positive returns are associated with "buy recommendations," but that even greater negative returns are usually associated with "sell recommendations."

As to the issue of analysts' honesty in recommendations, this certainly is a matter of concern. In recent years there have been numerous instances reported in the popular news media of inappropriate recommendations resulting from conflicts of interest. For instance, there is considerable controversy around analysts' recommendations in the recent Enron scandal, as well as in other similar situations. This issue is a matter of concern for all investment managers who pay any attention to analysts' recommendations in their evaluation process.

VI: STUDIES OF INSTITUTIONAL PORTFOLIO PERFORMANCE

6.1 Introduction

The principal purpose of this chapter is to present in chronological order the findings of many of the more widely-cited studies in the area of institutional portfolio performance. These studies focus on conventional equity mutual funds, which account for approximately 25% of the equity holdings in the United States.[32] The papers primarily address the issue of return performance, which is the subject of the earliest research of pioneering authors, including Close (1952) and Jensen (1968). In addition, many of these studies also investigate market timing, security selection, and performance persistence, in the course of their analyses. The following three sections focus on performance, timing, and persistence, respectively.[33]

---

[32] Separate literatures address closed-end investment companies and pension funds. Investment company studies are not included because most investment company studies focus on discounts rather than on performance per se (see Anderson and Born (1992, 2002)). Pension fund studies are not included because of agency issues and related matters, as discussed by Snigaroff (2000). See Lakonishok et al. (1992) for a discussion of pension funds.

[33] For reference purposes, a sample of other works which tangentially address performance, timing, and/or persistence, are chronologically listed, with their topics briefly summarized in the chapter appendix.

6.2 Performance Findings

Prior to 1965, a mutual fund's performance was often rated by comparison to other funds' returns or by averaging returns for a number of periods. Improvements over these methods began with Treynor (1965) who, in "How to Rate Management of Investment Funds," presents a new way of viewing performance results. Treynor discusses both the market influence on portfolio returns and investors' aversion to risk. The article consists of three parts: (1) a presentation of the *characteristic line*, which relates a fund's expected return to the return of a suitable market average; (2) a presentation of the *portfolio-possibility line*, which relates the expected value of a portfolio holding a fund to the owner's risk preferences; and (3) a measure for rating management performance using the graphical technique developed in (1) above.

In 1966, Sharpe, in "Mutual Fund Performance," explains that the expected return on an efficient portfolio $E(R_p)$ and its associated risk (σ_p) are linearly related:

$$(1) \qquad E(R_p) = R_F + \beta\sigma_p,$$

wherein R_F is the risk-free rate and β is a risk premium. The optimal portfolio with the risky portfolio and a risk-free asset is the one with the greatest reward-to-variability ratio:

$$(2) \qquad \left[\frac{R_p - R_F}{\sigma_p}\right].$$

The author examines 34 open-end mutual funds (1954-1963) and finds Sharpe ratios ranging from 0.78 to 0.43. He provides two explanations for the results: (1) the variation is either random or due to high fund expenses, or (2) the difference is because of varying management skills.

In a seminal work two years later, Jensen (1968), in "The Performance of Mutual Funds in the Period 1945-1964," investigates performance with a model that statistically measures a fund's performance relative to a given benchmark. The equation is:

$$(3) \quad R_{jt} - R_{Ft} = \alpha_j + \beta_j (R_{Mt} - R_{Ft}) + u_{jt},$$

where the α is termed "Jensen's alpha." A positive α indicates superior security price forecasting. A negative α indicates either poor stock selection or the existence of high expenses. Jensen investigates 115 fund returns relative to the S&P 500 index, and finds that on average, funds earned 1.1% less than expected given their level of systematic risk.

The papers of Carlson (1970) "Aggregate Performance of Mutual Funds, 1948-1967," and McDonald (1974) "Objectives and Performance of Mutual Funds, 1960-1969," address performance relative to type and objective, respectively. Carlson shows that regressions of fund returns on the S&P index have a high unexplained variance which is significantly reduced when an appropriate mutual fund index is used as the market proxy. In a tangential vein, McDonald reports that aggressive portfolios appear to outperform less aggressive ones. However, the author examines mean excess return divided by standard deviation and finds that a majority of the estimated ratios fall below the ratio for the market index.

As opposed to earlier studies examining the actual returns realized by mutual fund investors, Grinblatt and Titman (1989), in "Mutual Fund Performance: An Analysis of Quarterly Portfolio Holdings," employ both actual and gross portfolio returns in their study. The authors report that superior performance may exist among growth funds, aggressive growth funds, and smaller funds, but these funds have the highest expenses, thus eliminating abnormal investor returns. In a follow-up 1993 study these authors introduce a new measure of portfolio performance, the "Portfolio Change Measure" and conclude with essentially the same findings.

In a comprehensive study "Returns from Investing in Equity Mutual Funds: 1971 to 1991," Malkiel (1995) employs every diversified equity mutual fund sold to the public for the period 1971-1991 to investigate performance, survivorship bias, expenses, and performance persistence. As taken from Anderson and Ahmed (2005):

> The author explains that several "cracks" appear in the efficient market edifice during the 1970s and early '80s. Among these for stock returns are: (1) positive and negative correlation among security returns over short and longer time periods, respectively, (2) several seasonal and day-of-the-week patterns, and (3) predictability of stock returns based on variables such as dividend yields, firm size, PE ratios, and price-to-book value ratios. Cracks that appear for mutual funds are: (1) managers' ability to generate returns slightly above the Capital Asset Pricing Model (CAPM) market line, and (2) past mutual funds' returns predict future returns.
>
> Malkiel investigates survivorship bias, performance, performance persistence, and expense ratios, respectively. He reports some impact of survivorship bias as seen in annual returns for all funds of 15.69%, compared to 17.09% and 17.52% for surviving funds and the S&P 500 Index, respectively. These findings contrast with those of Grinblatt and Titman, and Malkiel attributes this to the survivorship bias of those authors' fund sample. To consider performance he calculates the funds' alpha measure of excess performance using the CAPM model. He finds the average alpha to be -0.06%,

with a T-ratio of only -0.21, thus to be indistinguishable from zero.   Using the Wilshire 5,000 Index as a benchmark, he finds the alpha is negative with net returns and positive with gross returns, but neither alpha to be significantly different from zero. He also finds no relationship between betas and total returns.   Hence, investors seeking higher returns will generally not obtain them by purchasing high-beta mutual funds.

When investigating the persistence of mutual fund returns,   the   author   analyzes   predictability   by constructing tables showing successful performance over successive periods. Consistent with earlier studies, he finds that there is some fund return persistence during the earlier decade, but that this persistence does not hold during the second decade. From this he suggests that persistence may have existed earlier, but has since disappeared.   However, even when persistence existed during the 1970s, many investors would not have benefited from buying funds with a "hot hand" because of the load charges (up to 8% of asset value) entailed with their purchase.

In his analysis of expense ratios he finds a strong and significant negative relationship between a fund's total expense ratio and its net performance. He does find some evidence that investment advice expenses are associated with positive returns, but attributes this to a few outlying funds, which suggests that investors are not ultimately rewarded for money spent on investment advisory expenses. In the conclusion Malkiel holds that funds have tended to underperform the market both before and after all reported expenses (except loads). Malkiel documents the persistence phenomenon, but notes that it is likely the result of survivorship bias and may not be robust. He concludes that his findings do not provide any reason to abandon the efficient market hypothesis.[34]

Following Malkiel, Gruber (1996), in "Another Puzzle: The Growth in Actively Managed Mutual Funds," uses a sample of 270 funds (1985-1994) and finds that mutual funds underperform the market by 1.94% per year.   With a single index model the underperformance is 1.56%, and with a four-index model the underperformance is 0.65% per year.   Non-surviving funds underperform the market by 2.75% per year.   Gruber also tests index funds and reports that they have an average annualized negative alpha of 20.2 basis points, with average expenses of 22 basis points.

In a more recent, widely-cited paper by Wermers and Moskowitz (2000), "Mutual Fund Performance: An Empirical Decomposition into Stock-Picking Talent, Style, Transactions Costs, and Expenses," the authors decompose mutual fund returns by attributable factors such as stock holdings, expense ratios, and transaction costs. Findings indicate that annual trading costs are lower and expense ratios are higher in 1994 than in 1975. Furthermore, mutual funds on average hold stocks that outperform a market index by roughly their combined expenses and transactions costs, but the funds' net returns are about 1% lower than the CRSP index.

6.3 Market Timing Findings

In the earliest paper to directly address market timing Treynor and Mazuy (1966), in "Can Mutual Funds Outguess the Market?," explain that the only way a fund can translate ability to outguess the market into higher shareholders' returns is to vary the fund's systematic volatility in a manner that results in an upwardly

---

[34] pp. 35-37.

concave characteristic line.[35] Returns for 57 funds (1953-1962) are examined to determine if the volatility of a fund is higher in up-years than in down-years. They compute a characteristic line wherein a managed fund's return is plotted against the rate of return for a suitable market index.

The specific model used by Treynor and Mazuy to test mutual fund managers' market timing ability is stated:

$$(4) \qquad r_{p,t} = \alpha_p + \beta_p r_{m,t} + \mu_p r_{m,t}^2 + \varepsilon_{p,t},$$

where $r_{p,t}$ is the excess return on a portfolio at time t, $r_{m,t}$ is the excess return on the market, μ_p measures timing ability (if a mutual fund manager increases the portfolio's market exposure prior to a market increase, then the portfolio will be a convex function of the market's returns, and μ will be positive). They find no evidence of curvature in any fund's characteristic lines and conclude that none of the managers outguesses the market.

A decade after Mazuy and Treynor, Miller and Gressis (1980), in "Nonstationarity and Evaluation of Mutual Fund Performance," address the issue of market timing. They explain that estimated fund alpha and beta may provide misleading information if nonstationarity is present in the risk-return relationship and is ignored. They examine 28 no-load funds and find that only one fund has stationary betas, while the number of betas for any given fund varies considerably over periods. Their findings indicate both weak, positive relationships and weak, negative relationships between betas and the market return, hence little evidence of timing ability.

During the ensuing years, several widely cited articles address the issues of timing and securities selection. Kon and Jen (1979) in "The Investment Performance of Mutual Funds: An Empirical

---

[35] A model similar to the one used by Treynor and Mazuy was later developed by Henriksson and Merton (1981).

Investigation of Timing, Selectivity and Market Efficiency," employ several models of market equilibrium to evaluate simultaneous market timing and stock selectivity performance. Using a sample of 49 mutual funds with different investment objectives, they report that some funds generate superior selectivity performance but that fund managers are unable to select securities well enough to recoup research expenses, management fees, and commissions. These finding are supported by Kon (1983) in "The Market-Timing Performance of Mutual Fund Managers," who finds that a sample of funds produces better selectivity than timing performance. Like results are reported by Chang and Lewellen (1984) in "Market Timing and Mutual Fund Investment Performance," who jointly test for either superior market-timing or security-selection skills for a sample of 67 mutual funds during the 1970s, and find that managers' security selection abilities are significant in only five instances, and three of these five have negative values. Similar findings are reported for managers' market-timing abilities.

Ten years later, Ferson and Schadt (1996), in "Measuring Fund Strategy and Performance in Changing Economic Conditions," address the effects of incorporating informational variables in an attempt to better capture the performance of managed portfolios such as mutual funds. Their conditional models allow estimation of time-varying conditional betas, as managers are likely to shift their bets on the market to incorporate information about market conditions. Using 67 mutual funds over the period 1968-1990, they find that the use of conditioning information is significant. In contrast to traditional measures of performance, conditional models produce alphas that have a mean value of zero; thus there is no evidence of perverse market timing. In a similar vein, Ferson and Warther (1996), in "Evaluating Fund Performance in a Dynamic Market" use data for 63 funds and show that, unlike the unconditional models, funds do not usually underperform the S&P

500 Index on a risk-adjusted basis. Soon afterward Becker, Ferson, Myers, and Schill (1999), in "Conditional Market Timing with Benchmark Investors," investigate the market-timing ability of mutual funds by employing models that: (1) allow the manager's payoff function to depend on excess returns over a benchmark, and (2) distinguish timing based on public information from timing based on superior information.   Their conditional market-timing model yields no evidence of timing ability, which is more reasonable than that reported in the prior literature on market timing.

Volkman (1999), in "Market Volatility and Perverse Timing Performance of Mutual Fund Managers," investigates fund managers' security-selection and market-timing abilities over the 1980s, as well as performance persistence prior to and after the 1987 crash.   Using data for 332 funds (1980-1990), he finds negative correlation between a fund's timing and selectivity performance and concludes that during periods of high volatility, few funds correctly anticipate market movements, although many funds outperform the market via security selection.

6.4 Persistence Findings

Although earlier works such as Sharpe (1966) and Grinblatt and Titman (1993) report evidence of performance persistence, Hendricks, Patel, and Zeckhauser (1993) focus primarily on the persistence issue in "Hot Hands in Mutual Funds: Short-run Persistence of Relative Performance, 1974-1988."   The authors examine a sample of 165 funds to test for short-run persistence and find positive performance persistence for four quarters, with a reversal thereafter.   They report that poor performance persists over time and that this performance is more inferior than "hot hands" performance is superior.   In another study, "Do Winners Repeat? Patterns in Mutual Fund Return Behavior," Goetzmann and

Ibbotson (1994) employ data for 728 mutual funds (1976-1988) and consider two-year, one-year, and monthly gross and Jensen risk-adjusted returns. They find support for the winner-repeat question with both type returns for funds overall, and with growth funds separately. Top-quartile and lower-quartile funds experience the greatest return persistence.

In 1995 Malkiel, in "Returns from Investing in Equity Mutual Funds: 1971 to 1991," (summarized above) finds that there is some fund return persistence during the 1970s, but that this persistence does not hold during the 1980s. From this he suggests that persistence may have existed earlier, but has since disappeared. He explains that even when persistence existed during the 1970s, many investors would not have benefited from buying funds with a "hot hand" because of the load charges (up to 8% of asset value) entailed with their purchase. Similar findings are reported by Brown and Goetzmann (1995) in "Performance Persistence." The authors' analysis of fund data (1976-1988) shows that 1,304 past winners are repeat winners; 1,237 past losers are repeat losers; and 1,936 funds reverse roles. However, persistence is not found to be a result of a winning management style each year. It is seen that performance persistence is more likely due to repeat-losers than to repeat-winners.

In a different vein, Kahn and Rudd (1995), in "Does Historical Performance Predict Future Performance?," analyze funds' performance relative to a set of style indices rather than to a single index model, as is done in many earlier works. The authors employ 300 equity funds and a sample of taxable bond funds (1983-1993) for analysis. Out-of-sample period performance is regressed against the in-sample performance, and results show no evidence of persistence among equity funds but some evidence of persistence among fixed-income funds.

In a more comprehensive work Carhart (1997), in "On Persistence in Mutual Fund Performance," investigates the persistence issue using a sample of 1,892 equity funds (free of survivorship bias) from 1962-1993. As taken from Anderson and Ahmed (2005):

> Following a brief review of earlier works on fund performance persistence, Carhart investigates the persistence issue using a sample of equity funds (free of survivorship bias) from 1962-1993. The sample comprises 1,892 funds divided among aggressive growth, long-term growth, and growth-and-income categories. He employs two models for performance measurement: (1) the Capital Asset Pricing Model, and (2) his four-factor model involving excess returns on a market proxy and returns on factor-mimicking portfolios for size, book-to-market equity, and one-year return momentum.
>
> Initially, portfolios of funds are formed on lagged one-year returns and performance is estimated. With the CAPM model, post-formation excess returns on the decile portfolios decrease monotonically in rank and exhibit an annualized spread of approximately 8%, compared to 24% in the ranking year. In contrast, the four-factor model explains much of the spread among portfolios (the size and momentum factors account for most of the explanation). He reports that expenses and turnover are related to performance, with decile ten having higher than average expenses and turnover. It does not appear that fund size, age, or load fees account for the large spread in performance of portfolios. Thus, the strong persistence of short-run mutual fund returns is largely explained by common-factor sensitivities, expenses, and transactions costs.
>
> The author repeats the earlier analyses using two-to-five-year returns in assorted portfolios. Over the longer periods, only top and bottom decile funds maintain their

rankings more than would be expected randomly. Decile one funds have a 17% probability of remaining in decile one, and decile ten funds have a 46% probability of remaining in decile ten or disappearing.   He concludes that the spread in mean return, unexplained by common factors and fees, is primarily attributable to strong underperformance by funds in decile ten. Expense ratios appear to reduce performance a little more than one-for-one, and turnover reduces performance nearly 1% for every round-trip transaction.   The average load fund underperforms no-loads by approximately 80 basis points annually. There is only slight evidence that any mutual fund managers beat the market. Although decile one funds earn back their investment costs, most funds underperform by the amount of their expenses.[36]

In a different vein, Bers and Madura (2000), in "The Performance Persistence of Closed-End Funds," extend the vast literature on investment performance in the mutual fund industry to closed-end funds.   The strongest evidence for persistence is obtained for equity funds as opposed to bond funds. The authors report persistence in portfolio performance in the 12-, 24-, and 36-month periods. They tentatively conclude that the "sheltered" nature of closed-end fund managers translates into superior performance.

6.5 Summary

In this chapter we have briefly presented the findings of several of the more widely cited works in the areas of professional portfolio performance, market timing ability of mutual fund managers, and mutual fund performance persistence. Although

[36] pp. 43-45.

early studies assessing mutual fund performance determine abnormal performance by using Jensen's (1968) alpha, many later studies also use the size and book-to-market factors identified by Fama and French (1993), and the momentum factor incorporated into the assessment of fund performance (see Carhart (1997)). However, perhaps not surprisingly, more recent findings in the area of mutual fund performance differ little from early findings in that they also find that fund managers do not generally outperform the market, even if the "market" is proxied by using a variety of benchmarks.

In the area of market timing, many studies use the models of Treynor and Mazuy (1966) and Henriksson and Merton (1981) to determine whether fund managers can time the market successfully. More recently, this area of analysis investigates "dynamic" market timing models conditional on the performance of the market. Overall, the findings to date on market timing indicate that mutual fund managers, by and large, are unable to time market movements.

In the final section above, we focus on mutual fund performance persistence, which addresses whether fund portfolios that perform well (poorly) previously continue to perform well (poorly) in the subsequent period. Papers such as Carhart (1997) indicate that there is little performance persistence for mutual funds. Even though a variety of studies have modified tests of persistence based on benchmarks, models, time periods, and combinations of these, no study to date has presented substantial evidence that there is persistence in fund portfolio performance, with the exception of Bers and Madura (2000).

Over the last five decades the literature on fund performance, market timing ability, and performance persistence, has evolved around various attributes, such as models and benchmarks used and time period investigated. The basic results have not changed; it appears that: (1) fund portfolios underperform the "market;" (2)

fund managers in aggregate are incapable of timing the market; and (3) mutual fund investors are ill-advised to invest based on prior fund performance.

APPENDIX 6A[37]:
ADDITIONAL FUND STUDIES

6A.1 Performance

Written in 1987, the work "Mutual Fund Performance Evaluation: A Comparison of Benchmarks and Benchmark Comparisons," by Lehmann and Modest (1987), provides empirical evidence on whether the choice of alternative benchmarks effects the measurement of performance.

In a study focusing on non-surviving funds, Lunde, Timmermann, and Blake (1999), in "The Hazards of Mutual Fund Underperformance: A Cox Regression Analysis," investigate the relationship between funds' conditional probability of closure and their return performance.

In a different vein Indro, Jiang, Hu, and Lee (1999), in "Mutual Fund Performance: Does Size Matter?," explore the question, "Does size of fund have any adverse impact on the performance of a fund?"

Some studies shift to more detailed considerations of fund performance rather than overall modeling. For example, Dickson, Shoven, and Sialm (2000), in "Tax Externalities of Equity Mutual Funds," investigate how the after-tax performance of a mutual fund is affected by sales and redemptions, and by the accounting cost method used.

---

[37] Some of the information presented here is adapted from Anderson and Ahmed, (2005) and from Anderson and Schnusenberg (2005).

Tangentially, Jain and Wu (2000), in "Truth in Mutual Fund Advertising: Evidence on Future Performance and Fund Flows," investigate actions by fund managers and how they relate to performance by considering funds that advertised in either *Barron's* or *Money Magazine* between 1994 and 1996.

A popular question in recent years is whether socially responsible investing results in superior returns. Statman (2000), in "Socially Responsible Mutual Funds," finds that the Domini Social Index (DSI) beat the S&P 500 index by a small margin between 1990 and 1998. Statman concludes that socially responsible investing is not necessarily inferior to conventional mutual fund investing.

Baks, Metrick, and Wachter (2001) take a novel approach to mutual fund performance in "Should Investors Avoid all Actively Managed Mutual Funds? A Study in Bayesian Performance Evaluation." They focus on an investor's perspective using Bayesian performance evaluation wherein an investor chooses to invest in an active fund when the prior point estimate of alpha is positive

Kothari and Warner (2001), in "Evaluating Mutual Fund Performance," also expand existing methodologies in evaluating fund performance. Using simulation, they find that the power of tests based on Jensen's alpha, the Fama-French three-factor model, and the Carhart four-factor model, is less than optimal and often results in incorrect conclusions.

Bliss and Potter (2002), in "Mutual Fund Managers: Does Gender Matter?," expect female fund managers to be more risk-averse and less overconfident than men, but they find that female managers take more risks and outperform men (based on Sharpe ratios and alphas) over the 1991 to 2000 period.

Another paper investigating fund performance differences by characteristics is Chan, Chen, and Lakonishok's (2002) "On Mutual Fund Investment Styles." The authors examine whether mutual fund performance differs by the style of the fund. Using Carhart's four-factor model, they find that the alpha for growth managers is 1.2% larger than that for value managers over the period from 1976 to 1997.

In a set of two papers, Pastor and Stambaugh (2002), in "Investing in Equity Mutual Funds" and in "Mutual Fund Performance and Seemingly Unrelated Assets," modify existing performance methodology by incorporating non-benchmark (or "seemingly unrelated") assets. In the first paper, the authors develop a framework in which prior views about pricing models and managerial skill are incorporated into the investment decision through the use of benchmarks prescribed by the Jensen, Fama-French, and Carhart models and by several non-benchmark assets. In their second paper, the authors attempt to show that an estimate of either alpha or the Sharpe ratio can be improved with the use of non-benchmark assets, including a book-to-market factor and Carhart's momentum factor.

Do performance outcomes of teams of mutual fund managers differ from those of individual mutual fund managers? Prather and Middleton (2002) ask this question in "Are N + 1 Heads Better than One? The Case of Mutual Fund Managers." Using Jensen's alpha and four alternative benchmarks, the results indicate little evidence that team-managed funds outperform individually-managed funds over the sample period from 1981 to 1994 for 147 individually-managed funds and 15 team-managed funds.

In a related vein, the use of incentive fees for managers is the primary topic in Elton, Gruber, and Blake's (2003) "Incentive Fees and Mutual Funds." The authors investigate whether incentive fees affect mutual fund performance over the 1990 to 1999 period.

The issue of fees and fund performance is also addressed by Massa (2003) in "How Do Family Strategies Affect Fund Performance? When Performance-Maximization Is Not the Only Game in Town." The author investigates whether mutual fund companies attempt to attract investors through both performance and diversification of the mutual fund family.

Reminiscent of Indro, et al. (1999), the issue of economies of scale is addressed by Chen, Hong, Huang, and Kubik (2004) in "Does Fund Size Erode Mutual Fund Performance? The Role of Liquidity and Organization."

Cohen, Coval, and Pastor (2004), in "Judging Fund Managers by the Company They Keep," develop two new performance evaluation measures based on the idea that managers' skills depend on how closely their holdings resemble those of other successful managers.

Nanda, Wang, and Zheng (2004), in "Family Values and the Star Phenomenon: Strategies of Mutual Fund Families," investigate mutual fund performance in the context of mutual fund families.

Closely related to the study above is the one by Gaspar, Massa, and Matos (2005), "Favoritism in Mutual Fund Families? Evidence on Strategic Cross-Fund Subsidization," wherein they investigate whether mutual fund families strategically transfer performance across member funds to favor those more likely to increase overall family profits.

Reminiscent of Statman (2000), Bauer, Koedijk, and Otten (2005), in "International Evidence on Ethical Mutual Fund Performance and Investment Style," investigate the performance of 103 ethical mutual funds from Germany, the U.K., and the U.S. over the period 1990 to 2001. Using both the CAPM and the Carhart four-factor model, their results indicate that these funds do not outperform a matched sample of conventional funds over the full sample period.

6A.2 Timing

Grant (1977), in "Portfolio Performance and the 'Cost' of Timing Decisions," provides a context for investigating the implications of treating the systematic relative risk of an investment portfolio as a random variable. The author compares the performance of a managed portfolio and that of the relative benchmark under the assumption that beta and market return are not independent variables. He concludes by noting that the relationships investigated are significant both in theory and in application.

In "Assessing the Market Timing Performance of Managed Portfolios," Jagannathan and Korajczyk (1986) discuss earlier reported puzzling evidence that funds exhibiting significant timing characteristics show negative performance more frequently than positive performance. The authors demonstrate both theoretically and empirically that portfolios can be constructed to show artificial timing ability when no real ability exists.

Bollen, and Busse (2001), in "On the Timing Ability of Mutual Fund Managers," extend the previous literature on market timing by examining daily (instead of monthly) data and by comparing the timing ability of mutual fund managers to a synthetic sample that exhibits no timing ability by construction.

Jiang (2003) develops a new, nonparametric measure of timing ability in "A Nonparametric Test of Market Timing." The new measure, theta is employed in an empirical test data (1980-1999) from both *Morningstar* and CRSP and 1,827 surviving funds and 110 dead funds. The author reports that the relationship between market timing ability and fund characteristics in the study is weak.

Sapp and Tiwari (2004), in "Does Stock Return Momentum Explain the 'Smart Money' Effect?," investigate whether the "smart money" effect can be explained by momentum, since Gruber (1996) does not control for Carhart's (1997) momentum factor when he documents the smart money effect.

6A.3 Persistence

Hendricks, Patel, and Zeckhauser (1997), in "The J-shape of Performance Persistence Given Survivorship Bias," discuss that social scientists must generally base their inferences on observations of non-experimental information, thereby presenting a challenge to unbiased robust inference from this data. The authors employ a simple regression-based approach to discriminate between a j-shaped pattern of persistence performance and a monotonic persistence in performance. They conclude that mutual funds exhibit a monotonic increasing pattern effected by true performance persistence.

ter Horst and Verbeek (2000), in "Estimating Short-Run Persistence in Mutual Fund Performance," recognize that previous techniques to estimate performance persistence may result in spurious confirmations of persistence because they regress a sample of funds' current returns upon a series of lagged returns. Another potential bias in estimating mutual fund persistence is investigated by ter Horst, Nijman, and Verbeek (2001) in "Eliminating Look-Ahead Bias in Evaluating Persistence in Mutual Fund Performance," which focuses on look-ahead bias.

In a study by Berk and Green (2004), "Mutual Fund Flows and Performance in Rational Markets," the authors develop a model showing that investments with active managers do not outperform passive benchmarks because investors competitively supply funds to managers and there are decreasing returns for managers in deploying their superior ability.

VII. STUDIES OF INDIVIDUAL PORTFOLIO PERFORMANCE

7.1 Early Findings

Early studies that address the individual in the investments arena are those by authors including Blume, et al. (1975) and Cohn, et al. (1974), among others, who deal with institutional issues such as the relative role of individuals versus institutions and issues of risk aversion in financial markets. Yet other studies of interest address tax issues.

In a different vein, one of the first studies that focuses on individual investors' performance is "Realized Returns on Common Stock Investments: The Experience of Individual Investors" (1978) by Schlarbaum, Lewellen, and Lease. In this work the authors focus on the individual securities transactions for a sample of roughly 2,500 retail investor brokerage accounts over the period 1964-1970 that made approximately 180,000 common stock trades. The authors analyze those "roundtrip" trades, that approximate 75,000 in number, or roughly 80% of all equity transactions. The vast majority of these trades are long positions, and 75% are round-lots. For each completed roundtrip, both a pre- and post-transactions-cost realized rate of return is computed.

After a discussion of their methodology the authors turn their attention to trading patterns and report "a mean investment cycle duration of approximately 8½ months and a median of 4 months" for their sample. (It should be noted that approximately 80% of the trades are roundtrip; thus one-in-five roundtrips are not completed.) They report that the most active 10% of investors account for 57% of the roundtrips and the least active 10% account for less than 1% of the trades.

Next, they report that the raw returns for roundtrip trades are 9.9% annually and 5.5% annually for pre- and post-transactions costs (see Table 7.1). Commissions and fees consume approximately 44% of the returns earned over the entire period, with short-term consumption being 63%, compared to 26% for roundtrips lasting more than one year. They report a strong inverse relationship between the length of a roundtrip and the annualized return rate earned on the trade.

Table 7.1: Relationship of Transaction Costs

All Round Trips	
Mean Rates of Return:	
1. Before Costs (%)	9.9
2. After Costs (%)	5.5
Median Rates of Return:	
1. Before Costs (%)	8.3
2. After Costs (%)	6.2

After their discussion of returns, they turn to the issue of benchmarking. For this purpose they employ seven different test portfolios, including both a value-weighted composite of NYSE and ASE stocks, and an equal-weighted portfolio of NYSE, ASE, and OTC securities. Note that the average annual return for the first benchmark is 6.9%, compared to 14% for the second. As reflected in Table 7.2, the authors compare the after-transactions-costs realized investor returns with corresponding-period returns for the NYSE/ASE value-weighted portfolio. It is evident that the performance differential pictures a much less positive view of the individual investors' management skills, especially considering that no allowance for transactions costs are made for the market portfolio.

Table 7.2: Comparison between the After-Transactions Costs Realized Rates of Return on Investment Round Trips and Corresponding-Period Rates of Return NYSE/ASE Value-Weighted Portfolio (%)

Round-Trip Category	Post-Transactions-Cost Annualized Performance Differential	
	Mean	Median
All Round Trips	.9	.5
0 – 30 days	35	24
31 – 182 days	1.4	.3
183 – 365 days	1.0	2.0
Over 365 days	.1	.2

Table 7.3 gives gross differential rates of return using the equal-weighted benchmark. Here, an even less favorable assessment emerges as the sample would be characterized as underperforming the market and especially so over longer time periods. The authors consider such a comparison to be a curiosity rather than particularly meaningful.

Table 7.3: Differences between Before-Transactions-Costs Rates of Return of Actual Investment Round Trips and Similarly Timed Round Trips with Equal Dollar Investments in All NYSE and ASE Securities (%)

Round-Trip Category	Equal-Weighted Index Annualized Performance	
	Mean	Median
All Round Trips	-1.7	-5.2
0 – 30 days	100	63
31 – 182 days	5.3	1.7
183 – 365 days	-.2	-.2
Over 365 days	-5.1	-6.4

In concluding, the authors state that individual investors display an overall picture of respectable investment acumen, especially in their short-term trading. Their rationale for such results is conjectural, and they speculate that this may result from trading responses to temporary securities price disequilibria. It may be that small investors can trade under these circumstances better than larger institutional investors, which might eliminate profit opportunities via their large-block transactions. Another speculation put forth is that the high quality of brokerage house recommendations to retail customers allows these customers to outperform the market.

The same authors, in a related paper, "The Common-Stock-Portfolio Performance Record of Individual Investors: 1964-70," compare the investment performance of individuals and institutions. They employ the same data set as above in contrasting individual investor returns with both naively-selected portfolios of similar risk profiles and with investments in mutual funds. The data comprise roughly $100 million of equity positions in portfolios approximating $40,000 each.

For the 84-months under consideration, the authors reconstruct the beginning-of-month portfolio balances for approximately 2,500 customer accounts. Four rate-of-return series are then constructed for the aggregated portfolios, as well as for four comparable benchmark collections of securities, and one series for mutual funds. Table 7.4 shows the annualized returns for after-transactions costs equal-weighted and value-weighted portfolios, as well as for the market benchmark and for mutual funds. As can be seen, there is little difference in the four series.

Table 7.4: Rate of Return Series: 1964-70.

Series	Rates of Return Annualized
A. Individual investor portfolio returns:	
(1) Portfolios equal-weighted:	
Actual trade basis, after transaction costs	8.73%
(2) Portfolios value-weighted:	
Actual trade basis, after transaction costs	8.60%
B. Market benchmark portfolio returns	
Value-weighted portfolio of capital NYSE/ASE stocks	8.09%
C. Equal-weighted mutual fund portfolio	8.99%

In further analysis the authors use a two-factor version of the market model and are unable to find alphas significantly different from zero. Thus, neither mutual funds nor individual investors appear to either outperform or underperform the overall market. In light of these findings, the authors conclude that perhaps one reason individual investors manage their own portfolios is because of the enjoyment they receive from doing so. This is consistent with their finding via questionnaires that investors enjoy the responsibility and challenge of securities management.

7.2 Taxes

In a different vein, but also of interest pertaining to individual investor behavior, is the issue of taxes. The literature on taxes as related to investing is broad, as evidenced by, among others, the earlier works of Dyl (1977), Branch (1977), and Reinganum (1983), who address year-end market behavior, tax trading rules, and the January effect, respectively. However, one of the first works to directly address tax-loss selling by investors at year-end is "Evidence on Tax-Motivated Securities Trading Behavior" by Badrinath and Lewellen (1991). In this work the authors explain that earlier inquiries into this arena, such as those of Constantinides (1984) and Chan (1986), have been largely inferential. Next, they proceed with an analysis of investor timing as to the realization of capital gains and losses from stock investments. The data employed comprise records of over 80,000 "round trip" investments in stocks by approximately 3,000 customers of a large brokerage house during the period 1971-1979. These data allow them to directly observe when heavy loss-taking activity by investors occurs. Table 7.5 shows that the number of losses realized (12,340) in the fourth quarters over the period far exceed the number of gains realized (7,513). As seen in the table, the profile of gains to losses over a year reflects an increase in the frequency of losses taken and a decrease in gains realized. In their conclusion they discuss that this pattern holds for investments which qualify for both short- and long-term gains treatment. They also report that a reduced tax rate on long-term gains and losses affects the timing of trades, but to a much lesser degree.

Table 7.5: Monthly Distribution of Realized Losses and Gains from Completed Investment Round Trips.

Month	Number of Losses Realized	Number of Gains Realized	Losses as Percent of Total
First Qtr	8860	12978	41
Second Qtr	9551	11189	46
Third Qtr	9634	9954	49
Fourth Qtr	12340	7513	62
Year Total	40385	41634	49

7.3 More Recent Findings

In "Are Investors Reluctant to Realize Their Losses?" (1998) Odean tests the disposition effect, which is the tendency of investors to hold losing investments too long and to sell winning investments too soon. The disposition effect was posited by Shefrin and Statman (1985) and is an extension of Kahneman and Tversky's (1979) prospect theory to investments.[38] The author also offers an alternative behavioral theory positing that investors may hold losers because they believe that these stocks will soon outperform today's gainers.

---

[38] Under prospect theory people behave as if maximizing an "S"-shaped value function, which is similar to a standard utility function that is defined on gains and losses instead of wealth. The function is concave in the gains domain and convex in the losses domain.

The author discusses tax-loss selling and explains that for tax purposes investors should postpone taxable gains while optimizing tax loss selling. After a brief discussion of related prior research the author tests 10,000 customer accounts' trades for the period 1997-1993. These tests investigate the frequency with which investors sell winners and losers relative to their opportunity set and also investigate tax-motivated selling in December. The primary finding is that for the entire year investors sell a higher proportion of their winners than of their losers. He also finds that the ratio of the proportion of gains realized to the proportion of losses realized for each month declines throughout the year. The proportion of gains realized declines from 2.1 in January, to 0.85 in December. The author performs additional tests and finds other interesting behavior, including that investors do not tend to buy additional shares of big winners. This finding is not consistent with a belief that small gainers will revert, but that large gainers will perform well.

In the discussion and conclusion the author summarizes that investors realize their profitable stock investments at a higher rate than their unprofitable ones in all months except December. Such investment behavior does not appear "to be motivated by desire to rebalance portfolios or by a reluctance to incur the higher trading costs of low priced stocks." The behavior is not justified by subsequent portfolio performance, which in reality exhibits lower returns, particularly for taxable accounts.

The next year, Odean in "Do Investors Trade Too Much?" (1999) discusses the difficulties encountered in determining at the macro- and micro-levels whether securities' trading volume is excessive. In theoretical models, trading models can range from zero to infinity, contributing to the difficulty of testing. The author's objective is to determine whether the trading volume of a particular subgroup of investors, those having discount brokerage accounts, is excessive. To do this the paper tests whether trading profits of these customers are sufficient to cover their trading costs. A sample of 10,000 accounts (1987-1993) is examined. In these accounts there are approximately 50,000 purchases and 48,000 sales. With average equally-weighted commissions of 2.23% and 2.76%, respectively, average turnover for these accounts is approximately 0.78 annually. To test for traders' ability to buy outperformers versus to sell poor performers, return horizons of 84 days, 252 days, and 504 days, following a transaction are examined. The null hypothesis that purchased securities outperform sold securities by at least 5.9% (trading cost) is rejected at the a percent level "if the average subsequent return of purchases minus that of sales minus 5.9 percent in the data set is less than the a percentile average return of purchases minus that of sales in the empirical distribution." Table 7.6 shows average returns following purchases and sales. To test whether the investors' underperformance is due to poor security choice, the author examines market-adjusted returns instead of raw returns. Table 7.7 shows the average market-adjusted returns following purchases and sales.

Table 7.6: Average Returns Following Purchases and Sales

	n	84 trading days later	252 trading days later	504 trading days later
Purchases	49948	1.83	5.69	-24.00
Sales	47535	3.19	9.00	27.32
Difference		-1.36	-3.31	-3.32
N1		(0.001)	(0.001)	(0.001)
N2		(0.001)	(0.001)	(0.002)

The rows labeled N1 give significance levels for rejecting the null hypothesis that the expected returns to securities purchased are 5.9 percent (the average cost of a round-trip trade) or more greater than the expected returns to securities sold.

Table 7.7: Average Market-Adjusted Returns Following Purchases and Sales

	n	84 trading days later	252 trading days later	504 trading days later
Purchases	49948	-1.33	-2.68	-0.68
Sales	47535	0.12	0.54	2.89
Difference		-1.45	-3.22	-3.57
N1		(0.001)	(0.001)	(0.001)
N2		(0.001)	(0.001)	(0.002)

In summary, the author reports that securities purchased not only fail to outperform securities sold by the amount of trading costs, but securities purchased on average underperform those that are sold. This holds even when trading is not obviously motivated by tax-loss selling, portfolio rebalancing, liquidity demands, or lessening portfolio risk. Surprisingly, even when trading costs are ignored, investors lower their returns via trading. The author suggests that:

> ...these patterns can be explained by the difficulty of evaluating the large number of securities available for investors to buy, by investors' tendency to let their

attention be directed by outside sources such as the financial media, by the disposition effect, and by investors' reluctance to sell short.[39]

In a follow-up article Barber and Odean (2000) analyze the investment activity of 166 investment clubs. Using data for the period 1991-1996, the authors show that the average club held 7.5 stocks worth $37,416, compared to the average individual in this data base who held 4.3 stocks worth $47,334. It is seen that the round-trip commission for clubs is 7%, which is higher than the 5% for individuals. The average club experienced a turnover ratio of 65%, compared to an average mutual fund or to individual investors with turnovers of approximately 76%.

The authors calculate four risk-adjusted measures of performance: (1) an own-benchmark abnormal return using the initial portfolio as a benchmark, (2) a mean monthly market-adjusted abnormal return utilizing NYSE/Amex/Nasdaq stocks, (3) an estimation of Jensen's alpha, and (4) an intercept test using Fama and French's three-factor model. For an index fund, individuals, and clubs, respectively, their results show annualized gross returns of 18.0%, 18.7%, and 17.0%, with net returns of 17.8%, 16.4%, and 14.1%.

The clubs show little ability to select securities, as the stocks they choose to sell generally provide greater returns than the stocks they choose to buy. For both clubs and individuals their gross returns are diminished by trading. The authors conclude that clubs encourage savings, educate their members about markets, and foster friendships, but do not beat the market.

Another work by Barber and Odean (2001) dealing with the issue of trading is "Boys Will Be Boys: Gender, Overconfidence, and Common Stock Investment." The authors explain that it is unlikely that the demands of rational trading activity account for

---

[39] See p. 1296.

the turnover rate of 76% on the New York Stock Exchange in 1998. They posit that overconfidence of investors may be a simple, yet powerful explanation for the high levels of trading in financial markets. After a discussion of overconfidence and trading, they propose to test whether overconfident investors trade more and realize lower average utilities by partitioning their data set on the basis of gender. Their two testable hypotheses are: (1) men trade more than women; and (2) by trading more, men hurt their performance more than do women.

For analysis, their data set includes approximately 29,000 accounts opened by men and 8,000 accounts opened by women, for which they estimate monthly returns from February 1991, through January 1997. Only stock transactions are of interest, and the monthly portfolio turnover is computed as one-half monthly sales turnover plus one-half monthly purchase turnover. They calculate an "own-benchmark" abnormal return which represents the return that an account would have earned by holding its beginning-of-year portfolio.

They find that women have portfolio turnovers of approximately 53% annually; while men's turnover rates are approximately 77%, thereby allowing them to reject the null hypothesis that these rates are similar for men and women.[40] The own-benchmark monthly returns for women are − 0.143% lower than the beginning-of-the-year portfolio, and for men this number is − 0.221%. It is also seen that stocks which both men and women sell earn significantly greater returns than the stocks they buy. The authors' findings allow them to state that men's greater trading activity, not poorer selection ability, is what lowers their returns relative to those of women. After a discussion of excess trading by

---

[40] Anderson and Stranahan (2005) analyze a dataset of 1027 full-service brokerage equity accounts (1998-1999) and find that, among all investors, the elderly, minority, and clients with less wealth, are the most likely retail brokerage clients to exhibit excessive trading activity.

mutual funds relative to excess trading by individuals, the authors conclude that overconfidence may be the simple explanation for the high trading activity exhibited by both groups.

7.4 Summary

Over the past three decades, several researchers have investigated the investment performance of individual investors. The early research of Schlarbaum, et al. reports that individuals overall display respectable investment acumen, as their portfolios perform in line with the overall market, as well as with mutual funds. In contrast, the later findings of Odean and of Barber and Odean indicate that individual investors tend to underperform the overall market. It is not immediately obvious why the earlier and later findings differ. However, one possibility is because of the earlier benchmarks used, as noted above. Regardless, it is seen that roundtrip commissions over both periods amount to roughly 5% of transactions prior to impact costs.

As to the later findings, these are attributable to both poor security selection and to excessive trading activity. However, suboptimal investment behavior is not equally distributed among investors, as men in particular, as well as certain demographic groups, tend to be more likely to trade excessively.

VIII. INVESTMENT COSTS AND THE MISMANAGEMENT ISSUE

8.1 Introduction

Investment costs are important because they reduce the benefits that an investor would otherwise receive. As has been seen in the prior two chapters, there are a number of cost factors in both the professional and individual portfolio management areas that can unfavorably impact an investor's return. However, even though these factors are relatively straightforward, their impact is not always easily identifiable. Thus, their manifestations as investment mismanagement may not be easily determined. In this chapter, the next section briefly reviews those facets of professional portfolio management identified in Chapter VI which may contribute to investment mismanagement. The third section addresses equivalent facets in the individual portfolio management arena. Section 8.4 analyzes the impact of mismanagement in an historical return context. The final section discusses costs in a mismanagement context.

Before proceeding, it is appropriate to acknowledge the obvious: (1) Professional investment managers must incur expenses and charge fees for their services; and (2) Individual managers must also incur expenses. Thus, the underlying question of interest concerns the value added relative to these fees and expenses. Are the fees and expenses excessive?

8.2 Institutional Portfolio Management Issues

As seen in Chapter VI, there have been numerous studies investigating fees, expenses, style issues, security selection, and market timing, in the area of mutual funds. Although the last three of these factors are well-defined, some studies lump together the various expenses associated with portfolio management. For the purposes of this chapter, sales charges and 12b-1 fees are referred to as "fees," and the term "expenses" is reserved for management fees and indirect expenses, such as portfolio commissions, style and timing factors, and market impact effects.

Loads and 12b-1 Fees

Fees essentially take two forms: sales loads and 12b-1 fees. Loads are commissions charged to mutual fund investors, which may be paid up-front, over-time, or at redemption. Sales charges which are incurred at the time of a mutual fund purchase have historically ranged upwards of 8.5%.[41] Today these charges are generally in the 4% range. However, there are also no-load funds on which no sales commissions are paid. The other distribution fee, the 12b-1 fee, is a relatively recent phenomenon originating in the 1980s, which is paid annually by shareholders,[42] These fees were introduced by the industry in an attempt to thwart share redemptions by investors.

Both of the above factors are investigated by Dellva and Olson (1998) in "The Relationship Between Mutual Fund Fees and Expenses and Their Effects on Performance." In this study the authors examine the issue of fees, including front-end loads, redemption fees, and 12b-1 fees. They report that front-end load funds have lower risk-adjusted returns and that 12b-1 fees, along with deferred sales charges and redemption fees, on average

---

[41] Although these fees could be addressed in the following section, they are included here because they are levied by the fund industry.

[42] 12b-1 fees, which usually amount to 0.25% annually, are paid via a direct reduction of net asset value.

increase expenses.   In another study addressing loads, Carhart
(1997) reports that the average load fund over the 1962-1993 period
underperforms no-load funds by approximately 80 basis points per
year.

In a different vein, McLeod and Malhotra (1994) explain that
12b-1 proponents often argue that these plans should result in: (1)
additional growth providing economies of scale, (2) continuous in-
flows for facilitating redemptions, and (3) a method for payment for
services.   Opponents argue that the payments are really sales
charges. The authors employ data from 1988-1999 and find that
funds with 12b-1 plans have higher expense ratios than those that do
not have a plan, thus, contributing to the evidence that the plans are
dead-weight costs to investors. In another study, the same authors
(1997) report a positive association between higher expenses and
12b-1 plans, as well as higher expenses for load funds.

As can be seen in the above studies, both loads and 12b-1 fees
apparently represent dead-weight costs to investors. When these
expenses are combined with the impact of management fees and
other costs as seen below, it is obvious that professional fund
managers face a Herculean task in generating returns that will allow
their investors (especially load fund investors) to reap returns
equivalent to those of passive benchmarks.

Management Expenses

In the first academic mutual fund article of which the author is
aware, Close (1952) in "Investment Companies: Closed-End
versus Open-End" foreshadows future interest in the area of
management fees and their impact on the holders of mutual funds.
He instructs potential investors to strongly consider management
fees when making choices in investment company selections. A
decade later, in another early study "Mutual Fund Management
Fee Rates," Herman (1963) discusses management fees relative to

several issues: (1) administrative services provided to the funds, (2) fund performance, and (3) fees and expenses incurred in servicing non-mutual fund clients, among others. The author concludes that the issue of management fees raises the question of whether shareholder interests are always best served.

Shortly thereafter, Sharpe (1966), in his path-breaking study, alludes to the impact of management fees on fund returns as a reason for the high variability in the cross-sectional variation of fund returns. Next, Jensen (1968), in his renowned performance study, is the first to specifically point out that on average market-adjusted mutual fund returns do not offset research expenses and management fees.

Decades later, Gruber (1996) reports that mutual funds (1985-1994) underperform the market by 1.9% per year, and the average fund's expense is 1.1% annually.[43] These numbers are consistent with those reported by Carhart (1997), who shows that expense ratios appear to reduce performance by a little more than one-for-one.

From the above representative studies, it appears that most mutual fund management-related expenses are dead-weight losses for investors. Some find it interesting that management expenses have risen over the years (to approximately 1.5% annually) in contrast to declining, as one might expect from technological innovation. (See Bogle (2005) for a discussion of increasing expenses.) In addition to management expenses, there are yet other management-related impediments to generating returns, as seen in the following sections on style, timing, and turnover.

---

[43] Management expenses, which are charged annually as a percentage of assets, may range from approximately 20 basis points for index funds to upwards of 2.5% for other types of funds. It must be noted that over the past 60 years, as reported by Bogle (2005), the average expense ratio has risen from 0.76% to 1.56%, for a change of 105%.

Style

The issue of style in the portfolio management arena involves the stratification of funds in order to analyze their performance relative to a set of style indices. One of the earliest authors to address this issue is Carlson (1970), who reports that mutual funds should be grouped by investment objectives before measuring their performance relative to the market. However, the most frequently cited study in this area is Sharpe's (1992) "Asset Allocation Management Style and Performance Management," in which he explains that style analysis consists of determining a fund's exposure to changes in major asset classes' returns.

Other studies related to style include the study by diBartolomeo and Witkowski (1997) "Mutual Fund Misclassification: Evidence Based on Style Analysis," which measures the impact of fund misclassification. They report that for their sample of funds, investors experience increased returns, but only because of additional risk assumed.

As is seen in various analyses of style, the ultimate impact to the investor is relatively small compared to the impact of the fees and expenses addressed in the earlier sections above. However, this impact is significant when portfolio returns are compared to passive index returns. In addition to the impact of style drift, other portfolio management issues, such as market timing and turnover, also impact returns and are addressed in the following two sections.

Market Timing

The issue of market-timing is one that has received considerable attention, both analytically and empirically, in the investments literature. This is an important issue because market timing activities may reduce investor returns as a result of commissions.[44] The predominant finding is that professional managers exhibit little ability to time markets.

In a widely cited work "Are Mutual Funds Market Timers?" Veit and Cheney (1982) investigate the effectiveness of mutual fund managers' market timing decisions. The authors develop a successful timing strategy as: (1) correctly forecasting "bull" and "bear" markets, and (2) making appropriate changes in the fund's risk exposure in anticipation of forecasted market movements. They test the null hypothesis that funds' alphas and betas are the same in both up and down markets and report that, on average, betas and alphas do not change significantly in up or down markets. They conclude that a large majority of funds demonstrate unsuccessful timing.

Similar findings are reported by Chang and Lewellen (1984) in "Market Timing and Mutual Fund Investment Performance." The authors employ a parametric statistical procedure that jointly tests for either superior market-timing or security-selection skills. None of their results provide evidence of collective portfolio management skill either at the micro- or macro-forecasting level.

Later studies employing conditional models to investigate market timing include Ferson and Schadt's (1996) study "Measuring Fund Strategy and Performance in Changing Economic Conditions." Here, the authors modify the traditional Jensen (1968) model, as well as the market timing models of Treynor and Mazuy (1966) and Henricksson and Merton (1981) to incorporate conditioning information. Ferson and Schadt's conditional models produce alphas that have a mean value of zero, thus removing the evidence of perverse market timing, as suggested by traditional models.

---

[44] The issues of security selection and market timing are generally investigated jointly in research works. As to the ability of fund managers to exhibit superior selection skills, the evidence is somewhat mixed.

Turnover

As explained by Brown and Vickers (1963) in "Mutual Fund Portfolio Activity, Performance, and Market Impact," portfolio turnover is generated by two forces: (1) the investing of new monies received by the fund, and (2) management's decisions to alter the current portfolio. From their study of turnover rates for the 1954-1958 period, the authors draw the conclusion that variations in fund portfolio turnover rates are not associated with variations in performance.

Decades later, Carhart (1997), in "On Persistence in Mutual Fund Performance," reports that expenses and turnover are related to performance, with the poorest performing funds having higher than average expenses and turnover. Expense ratios appear to reduce performance a little more than one-for-one, and turnover reduces performance nearly 1% for every round-trip transaction.

In another work, Wermers (2000), in "Mutual Fund Performance: An Empirical Decomposition into Stock-Picking Talent, Style, Transactions Costs, and Expenses," shows that trading activity in funds doubles from 1975 to 1994. However, the annual trading costs (per dollar invested in mutual funds) in 1994 is one-third their 1975 level. In contrast, the average expense ratio in 1994 is somewhat higher than in 1975. Of the 2.3% difference between the return on stock holdings relative to the net return, about 0.7% is attributable to lower average returns for the non-stock holdings component of the portfolio. The remaining 1.6% is split between expense ratios and transactions costs.

Total Mutual Fund Costs

Although total costs to mutual fund investors will vary widely, depending upon investors' actions and upon particular funds, the above reported findings allow us to estimate likely, typical costs for investors on average. For our purposes, load fees are assumed to be 4%, and 12b-1 fees are 0.25% annually. The cost of load fund underperformance is reported to be 0.8% annually, and management fees, as reported by Bogle and others, approximate 1.2% annually, exclusive of 12b-1 fees. As seen above, costs directly associated with style and timing issues are reportedly small. However, the cost of turnover can be estimated to be approximately 1% annually, on average, based on earlier studies in light of current fund activity levels. Thus, the average total expenses for investors in no-load funds is estimated to be approximately 2.5% annually[45] For investors in load funds, these total expenses are estimated to be in excess of 3% annually, inclusive of loads. Now, we briefly turn to comparable issues for individual investors.

8.3 Individual Portfolio Management Issues

As seen in Chapter VII, individually managed portfolios tend to underperform the overall market. According to the studies therein, the primary reasons for this performance are overtrading and sub-optimal trading decisions. Concomitant with overtrading is the negative impact of commissions, which are often onerously high at full-service brokers, and smaller, but of economic significance, at most discount brokers. As reported earlier by Odean (1999), the average turnover for retail brokerage accounts is approximately 0.8 annually. The average roundtrip expense approximates 5.8% when both commissions and market impact are

---

[45] This is consistent with Bogle (2005).

considered. Thus, on average, trading expenses approximate 4% annually for many individual investors.[46]

In a related vein, Barber and Odean (2001) report a higher turnover rate for men than for women. Anderson and Stranahan's findings support Barber and Odean's and also show that certain demographic groups tend to trade more frequently than overall market turnover rates. In addition to the overtrading exhibited by individuals, Odean (1998) shows that individual participants tend to make sub-optimal trading decisions. Evidence indicates that investors tend to sell winners too soon and hold losers too long. Now, we turn to an examination of the potential impact of mismanagement in a costs perspective.

8.4 The Impact of Costs

This section presents an analysis of the impact of investment expenses in an historical return context. Because this book focuses on equity management topics, the statistic employed here as a benchmark is the 75-year geometric return of approximately 11% for equities. The impact of costs via mutual funds is first considered. This is followed by a comparable analysis for individuals' investment management. Table 8.1 presents the historical return, a gross 15-year terminal value, and various fee-adjusted terminal values. These fee-adjusted values (net profits) are shown relative to the ultimate impact of industry costs on investor returns generated over an assumed 15-year horizon. As is seen, an investor in an index fund would have profited by approximately $359,000 and foregone approximately $19,000 in profits because of fees and expenses. This may be compared to the investor in a typical fund (2.5% expenses), who would have

---

[46] Two other issues which have received only cursory consideration in the literature to date are under-diversification and margin-trading.

received approximately $240,000 in profits and ultimately foregone $138,000 because of fees and expenses.

Table 8.1: Investor Net Profits vs. Industry Costs Impact
(11% return over 15 years)

		Investor	Industry
Beginning Investment	$100,000		
Gross After 15 Years	$478,459		
Annual Expenses		Net Profits*	Costs Impact**
Index Fund (0.3% fee)		$359,425	$19,034
Annual Expenses (1%)		$317,725	$60,734
Annual Expenses (2.5%)		$239,974	$138,485
Annual Expenses (3.5%)		$195,888	$182,571

*Investor net profits computed as (Gross After 15 Years – Beginning Investment) – Fees.
** Industry costs impact computed as (Gross After 15 Years – Beginning Investment) – Investor Net Profits.

In a second scenario, the impact of industry costs is examined for individual investors who use either discount or full-service brokers. For our purposes we assume a one-way commission of 2%, which conservatively approximates retail commissions frequently charged by full-service brokers (1% assumption for discount brokers). If a retail full-service account has a turnover ratio of 0.8, then the expected commission expense is 3.2% (0.8 x 2 x 0.02), which when combined with an impact expense of 0.2%, equals a 3.4% total annual expense.[47] If we consider this retail investor with a turnover rate of 1.6, then the expected commission expense is 6.4% with an impact expense of 0.4%, for a total of 6.8% in costs. Table 8.2 presents the historical return, a gross 15-year terminal value, and various fee-adjusted terminal values. As seen, the total impact costs resulting to a hypothetical investor are highly significant, whether the investor utilizes a discount or a full-service broker.

[47] See Bessembinder (2003) for a discussion of market impact costs.

Table 8.2: Investor Net Profits vs. Industry Net Receipts
(11% return over 15 years)

		Investor	Industry
Beginning Value	$100,000		
Gross After 15 Years	$478,459		
		Investor	Industry
Annual Expenses		Net Profits*	Net Receipts**
Discount Broker Costs			
Turnover Ratio 0.8 (1.8%)		$274,403	$104,056
Turnover Ratio 1.6 (3.6%)		$191,786	$186,673
Full-Service Broker Costs			
Turnover Ratio 0.8 (3.4%)		$200,043	$178,416
Turnover Ratio 1.6 (6.8%)		$85,360	$293,099

* Investor net profits computed as: [Beginning Value *(1 + Rate of Return – Industry Costs) [15]] – Beginning Value.
** Industry costs impact computed as (Gross After 15 Years – Beginning Value) – Investor Net Profits.

8.5 Discussion

As is seen above, the impact of industry costs on mutual fund investors' profits can vary widely under a variety of investment scenarios which are considered acceptable in today's investment arena. For example, over a representative 15-year period, an investor in a typical no-load fund would have received $240,000 in profit from an initial $100,000 investment. However, the same investor would have received a profit of $360,000 by being in an index fund, or a profit of $317,000 in a fund with costs of 1%. The investor's choice of a typical load fund would have generated an approximate profit of $196,000.

In the case of a typical individual investor utilizing a full-service broker over the 15 years, the investor would have profited by approximately $200,000 on a $100,000 initial investment, but would have foregone $178,000 in profits owing to the impact of industry costs. This same investor would have profited by an additional $74,000 if the trades had been made at a discount house charging a 1% commission. However, if the investor had traded twice as actively as average at the full-service house, the net profit would have been $85,000, compared to the $293,000 foregone because of industry costs impact.

Now, we address the construct of mismanagement. In the context of the professional investment management provided by mutual funds, it is seen that, on average, most funds return to their shareholders less than would passively-managed funds. The costs generated by these actively managed funds are substantial in their impact on investor returns, as seen above. This has been especially the case with load funds, which charge sales fees and historically have underperformed no-load funds. It appears that, on average, investors receive little or no benefit from paying higher costs for professional fund management. So, in the case of professional investment management, the author leaves the reader with two questions: (1) Are mutual funds culpable of mismanagement when they charge fees that are substantially in excess of index fund fees and yet consistently underperform the indexes? and (2) Are individual investors guilty of mismanagement by purchasing actively managed funds for their own accounts or for those of their clients?

In a second vein, we consider the mismanagement issue in the case of investors who manage their portfolios through either discount or full-service brokers. As shown above, the ultimate impact of commissions and trading costs can substantially reduce investor profits. As reported by Schlarbaum, et al. (1978), investor returns over the 1964-1970 period were reduced by approximately 44% because of these costs. (Market returns averaged 10% annually over this period). These numbers are supported by the impact of costs, as seen in Table 8.2 above, for typical investors using full-service brokers. So, in the case of individual investment management, the author leaves the reader with two additional questions: (1) Are individual investors mismanaging their portfolios when they actively manage them, especially when employing the service of full-service brokers? and (2) Should individual investors actively manage their portfolios when the impact of management costs, even at typical discount brokerages, make it highly probable that they will underperform market indexes? In light of these questions, we now turn to the issues of suitability and appropriate account activity in the chapters that follow.

IX: SUITABILITY

9.1 Introduction

Overall, securities fraud is among the most frequent and costly of types of white collar crime and was on the order of $40 billion in the year 2000 (FBI (2002)). Such fraud encompasses a wide gamut ranging from contemporary "bucket-shop" operations, to the misappropriation of assets, to the more subtle issues addressed in this and the following chapter – suitability and churning. None of these factors are of recent origin, as there is ample evidence in the historical literature citing their routine occurrence throughout our financial heritage. Although there are currently rules and regulations which attempt to address these problems, especially in our areas of interest (suitability and churning), these violations of the public trust continue apace. Arbitrations involving such stockbroker misconduct have risen steadily in number and in magnitude over the past decade (SEC (2002) and Feldman (2001)).

Before proceeding to the articles of interest, it is appropriate to address the issue of brokers' responsibilities to clients as is laid out in the rules of the New York Stock Exchange (NYSE) and of the National Association of Securities Dealers (NASD). These rules are of utmost importance in the securities industry today, as well as when they were written and modified over the decades of the last century.

9.2 Self-Regulatory Organizations' Rules

The requirement that a financial advisor recommend proper investments has several sources, primarily in the rules of the Self-Regulatory Organizations (SROs). As an example, the NYSE requires that each member "know [his or her] customer" with respect to recommendations, sales or offers; this directive contains an implicit duty of the financial advisor that recommendations reasonably relate to the needs revealed by the customer's particular situation.   Also, the National Association of Security Dealers (NASD) has rule number 2300, "Transactions with Customers," which includes "Conduct Rule 2310, Recommendations to Customers (Suitability)" that requires a financial advisor to have reasonable grounds for believing that an investment is suitable and that reasonable efforts be made to obtain information concerning the customer's financial status and investment objectives, and other reasonable information before recommending a particular investment. In the 2001 *NASD Securities Manual* the rule states:

> (a) In recommending to a customer the purchase, sale or exchange of any security, a member shall have reasonable grounds for believing that the recommendation is suitable for such customer upon the basis of the facts, if any, disclosed by such customer as to his other security holdings and as to his financial situation and needs.

> (b) Prior to the execution of a transaction recommended to a non-institutional customer, other than transactions with customers where investments are limited to money market mutual funds, a member shall make reasonable efforts to obtain information concerning:

>> (1)   the customer's financial status;
>> (2)   the customer's tax status;
>> (3)   the customer's investment objectives; and
>> (4)   such other information used or considered to be reasonable by such

> member or registered representative in
> making   recommendations   to   the
> customer.[48]

Also under Rule 2300, the important issue of trading in mutual fund shares is addressed. The manual specifically prohibits trading in mutual fund shares because "these securities are not proper trading vehicles..."

If a financial advisor violates any of the rules, the SRO may institute a disciplinary action, although these have been infrequent. However, if the financial advisor's actions violate rule 10b-5, the general securities antifraud rule promulgated under section 10(b) of the Securities Exchange Act of 1934, or common law fiduciary duties, the client has a potential private right of action that might result in an award of damages against the financial advisor. We now turn to a primary article in the area of suitability.

9.3 "Defining Suitability"

In the article "Defining Suitability" by Anderson and Winslow (1992), the authors first review the practical and legal issues of suitability and churning. Following that, they develop an argument in a modern portfolio theory context in which they attempt to facilitate the determination of suitable investment activity. In their introduction they state:

> The ordinary investor normally looks to a broker to give
> advice regarding suitable investments. For that reason,
> the issue of the suitability of such investments is a
> fundamental part of the investment process and is
> important to investors and brokers alike. Suitability

---

[48] p. 4261.

> concerns the type of investment vehicles that an investor
> will utilize to attain investment goals that may range
> from rampant speculation to simply maintaining the real
> value of a pool of funds.[49]

They explain that over the past two decades, changes in the securities markets and in financial products have been enormous. Trading in conventional options and futures has expanded, while at the same time newer investment vehicles such as index options and junk bonds have appeared. Along with these changes, there have also arisen greater opportunities for abuse of investors by unscrupulous financial advisers.

The authors cite a well-known case in which a widow had her account churned with unsuitable investments until the account had less than half its original principal amount. This occurred because the broker placed her funds in an actively-traded commodity account. The widow was left with less money than she required for maintaining her lifestyle. This illustrates the real problem with unsuitable investments: an investor can lose not only more money than anticipated, but often more money than the investor can in fact afford to lose.

They proceed to discuss the practical significance of suitability by giving an overview of its legal consequences. They explain that the requirement that a broker recommend suitable investments has several sources, primarily in the rules of the Self-Regulatory Organizations (SROs). As noted above, the NASD has in its "Rules of Fair Practices" a rule ("Recommendations to Customers") requiring that a broker have "reasonable grounds" for believing that an investment is "suitable" and that he make "reasonable efforts to obtain information concerning . . . the customer's financial status . . . [and] investment objectives" and other reasonable information before recommending a particular

---

[49] p. 105.

investment. The NYSE requires that each member "know [his or her] customer" with respect to recommendations, sales or offers; this directive contains an implicit obligation for the broker to insure that the recommendations reasonably relate to the needs revealed by the customer's particular situation.   If a broker violates a suitability rule, the SRO may institute a disciplinary action or the broker may be subject to a lawsuit. Anderson and Winslow continue with:

> But if the broker's actions in failing to recommend suitable securities can also be found to violate rule 10(b), the general securities antifraud rule promulgated under section 10(b) of the Securities Exchange Act of 1934, or common law fiduciary duties, the client has a potential private right of action that might result in an award of damages against the broker.[50]

The authors then discuss some problems in reaching a conclusion regarding suitability. First, they explain that it is often difficult to separate suitability problems from churning violations because the two types of broker misbehavior often occur in the same case. This may happen because it is easier to churn an account with unsuitable, speculative investments that are not appropriate for the client.

Second, they explain that even when suitability issues do come to the forefront, further difficulties present themselves. As noted, some leading scholars have suggested that there is little to guide the matching of a client's needs to an appropriate level of risk and return. Also, customers may be overly aggressive in light of their circumstances, owing to their lack of financial sophistication.

Anderson and Winslow then explain that this generality problem is exacerbated by industry practices that confound a

---

[50] p. 107.

precise determination of suitability. As is frequently done with opening account statements, the broker's inquiry into the customer's situation and needs can result in the client's instructions being communicated in a manner too general or ambiguous to reliably indicate which investments might be suitable for that client's needs. One example may occur if the client is permitted to ask simultaneously for growth, income, and stability of principal. However, in their article, prior to pursuing this issue, the authors turn their attention to a brief overview of modern finance theory in an investments context and the basis for determining suitability.

In the section on modern portfolio theory the authors explain that a rational investor will assume incremental risks only if incremental returns can be expected. This basic idea is from utility theory, which describes the investor's likely utility from various combinations of risk and return. They use the risk-return paradigm to show that particular types of investments are suitable for certain investor objectives.

Figure 9.1: Investments Vehicles

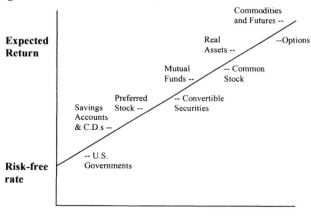

With Figure 9.1 they present the relative positions in risk-return space of a variety of investment vehicles. Government securities are the least risky. Savings accounts are considered less risky than corporate bonds, which in turn are less risky than preferred stock, etc. Futures and options can be viewed as the riskiest of financial assets.

The risk-return characteristics of an investment vehicle determine the suitability of that vehicle for an investor with a given objective. Fortunately, there are data available that show the historical risk-return relationship for the broad classes of financial instruments comprising the vast majority of investment vehicles. The arithmetic mean return for six groups of investment vehicles for the 1926-1987 period is shown in Table 9.1.

Table 9.1: Basic Vehicles: Summary Statistics Of Annual Returns (1926-1987)

Vehicles	Arithmetic Mean	Standard Deviation
Common Stocks	12.4%	20.4%
Small Company Stocks	17.5	33.3
Long-Term Corporate Bonds	6.2	8.6
Long-Term Government Bonds	5.8	9.4
U.S. Treasury Bills	3.8	3.1

As developed by Anderson and Winslow, the relative positions of different vehicles are approximate. Certain vehicles, depending upon their expected risk-return characteristics, are more appropriate for specific classes of investors. In Figure 9.2 they present a stereotypical view of where particular classes of investors lie in risk-return space.

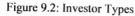

Figure 9.2: Investor Types

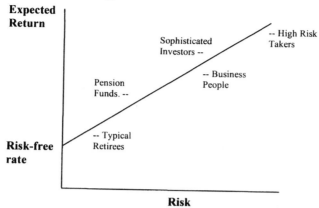

Following their treatment of suitable investments in a modern portfolio theory context, the authors discuss different mutual fund objectives and their respective investment vehicles as a proxy for identifying suitable investments for individual investors with given objectives. They explain that objectives of funds range from preserving principal via short-term government securities to speculating for large profits in the risky and volatile futures markets. As seen in Table 9.2, they describe the types of vehicles employed by the gamut of funds in various categories. They continue in discussing how an individual investor's objectives are likely to be consistent with a particular fund's objectives and that the vehicles appropriate for such individuals should be similar to those utilized by respective funds. It is from this plane that the authors call for a more thorough, objective standard for determining suitability.

Table 9.2: Fund Category and Investment Vehicles Held

Category	Vehicles
Aggressive Growth	Common stock in fast-growing, often speculative companies
Growth	Common stock in established growth companies
Growth-Income	Common stock in established growth companies, emphasizing dividend yield
Equity-Income	Common stock in mature companies, emphasizing dividend yield
Balanced	Common stocks and bonds in established companies
Income	Government or corporate bonds
Option-Income	Common stocks with emphasis on income and puts and calls
Small Company	Common stock in small, young companies

The authors explain that suitability issues may arise for several reasons:

> One reason for suitability problems may be that the customer did not clearly delineate his or her objectives to the account representative. Also, it is not uncommon for a customer to be unclear as to his or her own objectives. But the broker has the best chance to control the issue by thoroughly questioning the new customer... An examination of current practices reveals that brokers could do a better job of resolving suitability issues in individual cases. These current flaws lie in the information-gathering techniques currently employed by brokers and in the resultant communication failures between the broker and the customer concerning the latter's investment goals.[51]

They further discuss how several major firms' new account forms show a high degree of variation in the section of each firm's form

---

[51] p. 118.

addressing the objectives of the customer. For instance, Firm A's form asks the customer to rate in priority one or more of three objectives: (1) Income, (2) Growth, or (3) Speculation. It then asks the inventor to rate his investing experience as (1) None, (2) Low, (3) Moderate, or (4) High. This compares with Firm B's form which asks whether the customer seeks: (1) Appreciation with risk, (2) Speculation, (3) Income with safety, (4) Income with risk, or (5) Tax reduction, without specifying a priority requirement or a limitation on the number of boxes to be checked. After delineating related aspects of other firms' forms the authors state that the "only common element that the forms shared was that none asked the customer to describe the type of investment vehicles he or she would employ in attempting to reach his or her objectives." The authors contrast these practices with the more descriptive and varied types of investment objectives and associated investment vehicles that can be derived from the *Mutual Fund Sourcebook*.

The authors continue with a discussion of how the categories listed in Table 9.2 should be expanded to account for more speculative goals that require investment vehicles such as futures or index options. They suggest that categories (see Table 9.2 above) represent a better attempt at full communication than do the current practices of investment houses.

A further communication problem for some firms is then addressed. "Many brokers do not give the customer a copy of the agreement after the broker completes the new account form following an interview with the new customer. In any event, most brokers do not require the customer to sign the form. These are obviously poor practices." The authors summarize with:

> The potential for misunderstanding, or even abuse, presented by the use of such forms and procedures should be obvious. Such generality and open-endedness in categorizing 'investors'' objectives more readily allow the unscrupulous broker the opportunity to churn

an account using unsuitable vehicles that are too speculative in light of an investor's objectives. It also allows the broker to later argue that the customer's income objective was the basis for the broker's trading in high-yield junk bonds. Finally, if the customer does not see the broker's conclusions on the form, a greater potential for error is injected.[52]

They state that a law journal is not the best forum for designing reforms for the above practices, but that it is an appropriate forum to identify the problem and to advocate a policy position. The authors call for the NASD Board of Governors to evaluate this issue with two objectives in mind: (1) "the Board could consider the possibility of an interpretation or direction under its Rules of Fair Practice requiring NASD members to use a uniform new account form incorporating a less general 'objectives' section than most of those currently in use by firms," and (2) "the Board should require that the broker review the completed form with the customer, have the customer sign it when it is made final, and give a copy of the finished form to the customer." They conclude that these reforms should facilitate dealing with the issue of suitability.

---

[52] p. 120.

X: CHURNING

> The "customer's man" is the stock exchange's point of contact with the customer.[53] History teaches that the interest of customers' men lies in encouraging customers to buy and sell not only often but promiscuously and indiscriminately; ... to keep the customers' portfolios well churned so that by the quick inflow of commissions one may the sooner join the elite of high finance. (1940)
>
> William O. Douglas
> Member and Chairman
> Securities and Exchange
> Commission[54]

10.1 Introduction

As noted in the prior chapter, securities fraud is among the most frequent and costly of types of white collar crime and was on the order of $40 billion in the year 2000 (FBI (2002)). Such fraud ranges from contemporary "bucket-shop" operations, to misappropriation of assets, to the more subtle issues of: (1) suitability, which is the topic of Chapter VIII, and (2) churning, or a broker's excessive trading of an account for commission profits, which is the topic of this chapter.

The issue of excessive trading was early on addressed in the academic literature in a 1968 *Harvard Law Review* Note. This article generally addresses overtrading, as well as evidence of and

---

[53] At the time many of the references in this chapter were written, this was a male-dominated industry. Obviously, the current workforce is represented by both genders.

[54] Douglas, 1940, *Democracy and Finance*, pp. 107-109.

actions against the offense. Over the following years there have appeared other treatises addressing this issue, including a section in *Fraudulent Broker Dealer Practices* by Goldberg (1978). This work addresses the turnover metric (a measure of trading activity) of 6, proposed in the above *Harvard* Note as a hurdle rate for determining excessive activity. Goldberg's often cited 2-4-6 formulation posits that a turnover of 2 is active trading; a turnover of 4 is presumed to be excessive; and a turnover of 6 is conclusively excessive trading. However, in 1990 Winslow and Anderson offered a model suggesting that a more reasonable and justifiable standard of comparison for turnover is the rate for mutual funds with similar objectives to the account. Other works that review the various issues involving churning include that of Cantwell, et al. (1988), as an example.[55] For the purposes of this book we concentrate on the *Harvard* Note and the Winslow and Anderson article. Before proceeding to these articles in Sections 10.3 and 10.4, it is appropriate to first present a brief review of industry rules germane to churning.

10.2 Industry Rules

The issue of brokers' responsibility to clients is laid out in the rules of the New York Stock Exchange (NYSE) and of the National Association of Securities Dealers (NASD). The NYSE requires that each member "know [his or her] customer" with respect to recommendations, sales or offers; this directive contains an implicit duty of the financial advisor that recommendations reasonably relate to the needs revealed by the customer's particular situation. The NASD has rule number 2300, "Transactions with Customers," which includes "Conduct Rule 2310, Recommendations to Customers (Suitability)" that requires a

---

[55] See Poser (1984) for a discussion of options and churning.

financial advisor to have reasonable grounds for believing that an investment is suitable and to make reasonable efforts to obtain information concerning the customer's financial status and investment objectives, and other reasonable information before recommending a particular investment. Also under Rule 2300, there is a prohibition against trading in mutual funds because "these securities are not proper trading vehicles..." Although the manual gives no guidelines for determining overtrading of stocks, there exists Securities and Exchange Commission (SEC) Rule 15cl-7(a), as referenced in Jennings and Marsh (1987):

> It is unlawful for a broker, dealer, municipal broker, or municipal dealer to effect with or for a customer with respect to whose account he or his agent exercises investment discretion, or is in a position to determine the volume and frequency of transactions by reason of the customer's willingness to follow his or his agent's suggestions, transactions that are excessive in volume or frequency in light of the amount of profits or commissions of the broker, dealer, municipal broker, municipal dealer, or his agent in relation to the size of the account and such other factors as the character of the account, the needs and objectives of the customer as ascertained on reasonable inquiry, and the pattern of trading in the account.[56]

Although the issues of churning and suitability are frequently intertwined in court cases, it should be noted that suitability and churning are two distinct entities insofar as the first usually involves the appropriateness of investments for a particular situation, while the second involves excessive trading activity. However, because overtrading is more easily quantified than are issues of suitability, overtrading is more likely to be argued in

---

[56] p. 640.

arbitration than is suitability. Similarly, overtrading tends to be more frequently addressed in research articles than is suitability, as is evident in the following pages.

10.3 "Churning by Securities Dealers"

"Churning by Securities Dealers" is one of the first articles that addresses account trading activity in a churning context. In addition to examining the trading activity issue, this work also reviews the control basis for churning, as well as evidence of and actions against the offense. The article begins with:

> The 'churning' of a securities account occurs when a dealer, acting in his own interests and against those of his customer, induces transactions in the customer's account which are excessive in size and frequency in light of the character of the account.[57]

At that time, churning was primarily dealt with by the Securities and Exchange Commission via the general broker-dealer antifraud provisions of the securities acts, which prohibit dealers' use of any manipulative, deceptive, or other fraudulent practices. However, there were few recorded civil cases seeking recovery for churning. This is probably because potential plaintiffs were apparently unwilling to "throw good money after bad" by bringing lawsuits. Also, there was probably a tendency on the part of dealers to "settle many claims out of court in order to avoid unfavorable publicity and possible SEC sanctions."

As to the theoretical basis underlying churning, the article explains that a securities dealer is an investment counselor dispensing advice, "but he is also a salesman whose profits depend

---

[57] *Harvard* Note, p. 869.

on the volume of sales he makes." Hence, the conflict between these two roles results in a situation wherein customers may rely, to their detriment, on a dealer's advice when it is not disinterested; "it is this problem which the prohibition of churning is designed to meet."

The SEC's general concern with the fiduciary responsibility in the dealer's role is illustrated by the Commission's "shingle theory," under which a dealer is held to an implied duty when he "hangs out his shingle" that he will treat his customers fairly and honestly. In addition, as discussed above, the National Association of Securities Dealers also stresses the broker's fiduciary responsibility in terms more specific than those used by the SEC via the "suitability rule," which requires that a dealer have reason to believe that a recommended transaction is suitable for the customer's needs.

In the second section of the article, the elements of the offense are discussed. The first element is the dealer's control over the account. Dealer control over the transactions in an account is primary to a finding that the account has been churned, and the relationship between dealer and customer is an important indicator of such control. The SEC once limited its findings that churning existed to cases only in discretionary accounts, but now a degree of control can be inferred when the customer relies on the dealer's suggestions. Thus, control may be either direct or indirect depending upon the broker/client relationship.

When considering direct demonstration of control, the article states: "If the dealer has been handling the account and actively advising a customer for a long period of time, there may be an affirmative duty not only to recommend transactions which meet the customer's needs, but also to object to those which do not." It is explained that if all or most of the transactions in the account are made on the dealer's recommendation, control may be established directly.

In a related vein, if a customer leaves the business to the broker when out of town, this is regarded as strong evidence of control. Control is also indicated if the broker makes transactions for the account without prior authorization. Also, if a customer's complaints about the account's operation are met by soothing explanations but not accompanied by changes in the account, control may also be found.

In addressing the issue of indirect demonstration of control, the piece explains that naïve customers are those who are likely to follow the dealer's recommendations. However, there is an apparent lack of consistency in background among persons considered naïve, which suggests that "the 'finding' of naiveté is more a device used to justify a decision than a useful guide for future cases." However, there are several other factors which "the SEC will typically consider under the rubric of naiveté which relate more demonstrably to the likelihood that de facto control existed than does the customer's general background." Chief among these is the customer's previous experience in business and, more specifically, in securities matters.

In addition to naiveté as an indirect consideration of control, the relationship between the customer and the dealer is also important. According to the work:

> Reliance is very likely if there exists a close personal relationship between the customer and the dealer, especially one which antedates the business relationship, since the customer is likely to rely on that relationship as guaranteeing the disinterestedness of the dealer's advice. Because of this likelihood, the dealer will be expected to be scrupulous in his concern for the interests of longtime clients, personal friends, their widows, and, of course, his own mother.[58]

---

[58] *Harvard* Note, p. 873.

Following the discussion of control over the account, the article addresses trading in accounts. Once control by the broker has been established, it must be determined that the broker abused this control through an excessive amount of trading. The work explains that no single statistical criteria can establish churning, but that a view should be taken of the dealings in the account in light of its character. Since more activity can be expected in a short-term trading account than in an investment account in which a customer seeks conservation of principal and the receipt of income, more activity is necessary to determine churning in a trading account.

The article next turns to turnover, which is a measure of trading activity. This technique for determining excessive trading in an account computes the number of times the money invested in the account is "turned over," as usually measured by the total cost of all purchases over the period under consideration and divided by the "average investment." The article briefly reviews the findings of several cases in which the excessive turnover rates vary widely. "The most extreme case appears to be Shearson, Hammill & Co., in which one account was turned over 70.77 times over nine and one-half months...a turnover of approximately eight times each month. At the other extreme appears Behel, Johnsen & Co., in which the account was turned over four and one-half times in three years." It is noted that few cases involve turnovers of once per month, but that turnovers averaging once every two months have occurred more frequently. From this, the article concludes that complete turnover more than once every two months is likely to be labeled excessive.

There follows a discussion of "In and Out" trading, which is a pattern of trading with the money immediately reinvested in other securities, followed in a short period of time by the sale of the newly-acquired securities. "This conduct is extremely difficult for the dealer to justify." The article also states that excessive trading arises when dealers arrange for their customers to buy and sell from one another. This "shuffling" or "cross trading" is highly profitable for the dealer, "but it belies a claim that the trading decision was based on the merits of the security involved unless the dealer can demonstrate that the accounts had different purposes and that the security was suitable for one account but not another."

The article then points out that for the issue of dealer's profits there are no established standards for determining whether a dealer's profits are excessive. In this discussion it is concluded that the inquiry into the dealer's profits is not fruitful and "it may be doubted whether any substantial importance should be accorded to these profits as a separate consideration" in the context of churning.

As to the customer's profit as a defense against churning, many "dealers charged with churning have protested that the customer's account showed a net profit, but the SEC has consistently stated that this is not a sufficient defense." The piece explains that the term "profit" cannot be used in a vacuum but must be considered in relation to the account and related external variables. For example, a small profit made during a time of substantially rising security values should not provide a defense for the dealer. As well, a small loss while the market is in a substantial decline likely should not indicate dealer misconduct.

When considering government actions against churning, the writer states that by far the most frequent public proceeding against these dealers involves SEC disciplinary action. Although considerable space is devoted to this issue, it is not appropriate to summarize this section because today many of these issues are settled in arbitration.

In the final section, the work gives an overview of how determining the "proper measure of recovery in a churning action is complicated primarily by the difficulty of calculating what the customer lost as a result of the churning."

In theory, he lost the difference between what he would have had if the account had been handled legitimately and what he actually did have. But since it cannot be known what transactions would have been made in legitimate trading, it will never be possible to establish exactly the amount of his loss. Difficulties of measurement are not, of course, unique to the question of churning. Courts dealing with breaches of obligations by trustees are also forced to calculate damages caused by improper investments made over an extended period. Three measures for recovery against a trustee have been employed — quasi-contractual recovery of the profit made by the dealer, recovery for damages on an "out of pocket" measure, and recovery for damages on a loss of bargain measure — and each of these measures can be applied to churning cases.[59]

1. Quasi-contractual Recovery. — This recovery requires the return of profits or commissions earned by the dealer, and it is in part an application of the theory of unjust enrichment; dealers are required to return the fruits of their violations to the customer. The writer explains that this reasoning is inadequate because the dealer may have caused damage unrelated in amount to what was earned in commissions.

2. Out of Pocket Recovery. — This measure is preferable to quasi-contractual recovery in that its objective is to compensate the plaintiff. It may be computed as: (1) the difference between the amount of the customer's investment and the amount returned to the customer, or (2 the value of the original portfolio at market prices as of the end of the period under consideration less the final value of the account.

---

[59] *Harvard* Note, p. 883.

3. Loss of Bargain Recovery. — This measure attempts to cure the defects of the out of pocket measure by awarding the plaintiff the profits that a properly managed account should have yielded. The article explains that an arbitrary interest rate could be employed to calculate damages or an appropriate index might be used for proxy purposes. Obviously, as the work states, there are numerous potential problems inherent with this task

After a brief review of statutory limitations on recovery, the article concludes:

> ...the SEC has resolved many close legal questions in favor of protecting customers whose accounts show excessive trading and has imposed sanctions that should encourage dealers to take extensive precautionary measures to prevent future violations." Thus the Commission has reinforced its position that "securities dealers who are in a position to influence customers with their advice should bear some of the burdens of fiduciaries.[60]

10.4 "A Model for Determining the Excessive Trading Elements in Churning Claims"

In the abstract of this article, the authors explain that courts and commentators have long considered annual turnover rates to be a significant factor in evaluating the excessive trading element of churning claims. However, these authorities have lacked coherent guidelines for assessing the significance of investor objectives in the determination of whether a given turnover rate for a broker-managed investment account is excessive. The development of these guidelines is the primary focus of this work.

---

[60] p. 886.

In the introduction, they state that the churning of an investment account occurs as when a broker over-trades the securities in the account for the purpose of generating commissions. The authors review the three elements to recover under a churning claim: "(1) 'control' over the account by the broker; (2) excessive trading in the account in light of the customer's objectives; and (3) scienter, an intent to defraud or a reckless disregard of the customer's best interests by the broker." Of these three elements, excessive trading is likely the most difficult for plaintiffs to establish and the most bothersome for courts to evaluate.[61]

They explain that courts using quantitative turnover rates to measure the excessive trading issue have used them without satisfactory analysis in part because their analysis lacks a basis in financial theory. Historically, there is little of substance from cases as to why a particular rate is or is not excessive under differing investment objectives. "The symptoms of this lack of financial grounding have been imprecision and timidity in use of quantitative turnover rates as a factor indicative of excessive trading."

In their discussion of the background on churning, they explain that the brokerage industry's compensation structure rests on the volume of trading activity in customer accounts. Transactions conducted in customer accounts generate commission profits. Of these commissions approximately 30% to 40% flows directly to the individual broker who handles the account. Brokers employed by these firms generally receive compensation only when their customers trade in their accounts. "Because of this compensation system, both the firm and the broker enjoy a substantial financial benefit from increased trading activity in a customer's account, regardless of any gain to the customer from this trading." A broker

---

[61] p. 328.

thus possesses a terrific incentive to increase the frequency of trading in the customer's account.

The compensation structure creates one side of a potential conflict of interest situation for brokers regarding their customers; the other side is completed by the brokers' touting of themselves as "investment advisors." In addition, many large brokerage firms spend substantial sums advertising their investment advice as the best available. These efforts naturally cause customers to rely upon the firm's recommendations. The dual roles of commission salesperson and dispenser of investment advice present the broker with a conflict of interest: the temptation to generate commissions by advising that a security be bought or sold, irrespective of the customer's needs. "Given this potential for abuse by brokers, it is not surprising that litigation over alleged overtrading of customer accounts has long abounded."

In addition, greater incentives for brokers to churn customers' accounts have resulted from the enormous changes in the securities industry over the past 15 years. First, the introduction of competitive commission rates on May Day, 1975, has stimulated churning because of the declining profit margins experienced by brokerage firms. The increased competition has resulted in higher pressure on individual representatives to produce transaction business. Second, as noted earlier in the article, there has been an expansion in number and in complexity of the various types of investment vehicles that are available, thus increasing the alternatives for customer service and abuse.

The authors continue with: "A review of the current state of affairs indicates that the problem of churning has worsened in this most recent period." They explain that complaints to the Securities and Exchange Commission (SEC) about unauthorized trading, which often parallels churning, more than doubled from 1982 to 1984. Also, they observe that churning claims as well as other complaints against brokers are on the rise.

The authors next turn to a discussion of legal standards for churning liability, wherein they discuss the broad problem with turnover ratio analysis—the absence of any foundation in financial theory. As was pointed out in *Churning by Securities Dealers*, the rough rules suggested in many cases may be grossly and generally inaccurate for any category of investment. Thus, the legal rules used by previously referenced authorities seem grounded on an inappropriate arbitrary line drawing.

The authors continue: "This article attempts to ascertain a systematic relationship between the quantitative annual turnover rate and the qualitative objectives of the individual investor." It is proposed that the turnover rates for mutual funds with diverse investment objectives may be helpful in developing a relationship between the turnover rate and investor objectives "that is superior to that suggested by the authorities described in the preceding paragraphs." The following paragraphs give an overview of pertinent portions of modern finance theory, and then describe a study of turnover rates in mutual funds in order to define the relationship between investment objectives and turnover rates.

Because an individual investor's objectives depend upon the level of risk and return desired, it is reasonable to believe that accounts sharing similar investment goals may likely also share similar levels of trading activity. Courts appear to accept this proposition, as indicated by their statements that speculative or trading accounts should experience higher turnover than conservative accounts. Nevertheless, a reason that goes beyond the intuitive approach is provided by modern portfolio theory and the concept of the efficient frontier. With the efficient frontier an expected rate of return is associated with a level of risk for a particular investment portfolio. The points lying on the efficient frontier represent the portfolios that would maximize utility for different investors; investors with risk and return preferences will choose different points on the frontier.

As this concept applies to a portfolio of a rational investor, the broker handling the account will always seek to invest in a portfolio that lies on the efficient set instead of portfolios that offer a lower rate of return for the desired level of risk. However, because of the ever-changing marketplace, the maintenance of a position on the efficient frontier implies an optimum turnover ratio. Because commissions are a direct cost to the investor and are a function of turnover, they directly affect the return that a portfolio will generate, and costs in excess of the minimum amount necessary reduce the investor's return. Thus, one would expect that portfolios managed to lie on the efficient frontier will experience particular turnover rates.

The authors continue with a discussion of mutual funds as reference points for efficient portfolios because of the difficulties with direct use of the efficient set theory. They state that:

> Observing turnover rates for a sample of mutual funds with diverse, specific investment objectives provides a good opportunity to obtain data that approximates the location of points on the efficient frontier. While the use of mutual funds is an imperfect comparison, it is an informative source untapped for its full potential. At the very least, the turnover rates for mutual funds are representative of portfolios that lie within the efficient frontier, and, assuming that the mutual fund managers pursue the stated goals of the funds, the points will tend toward that frontier. Furthermore, mutual fund managers, unlike commission-rewarded brokers, lack the incentive to overtrade, and therefore serve as a natural test group, potentially associating optimum turnover rates with various investment objectives.[62]

---

[62] Winslow and Anderson, p. 344.

The authors offer several good reasons to support the proposition that the turnover rates of mutual funds will approximate the optimum turnover rates for broker-managed investment accounts. First, the mutual fund managers are professionals making investment decisions designed to maximize return for a given level of risk. In a similar vein, because of their fiduciary duties, brokers should strive to maintain a position on the efficient frontier by purchasing and selling securities in accordance with their clients' overall investment criteria. Second, the compensation of a mutual fund investment adviser is more closely tied to investment performance than trading activity, which determines a broker's compensation. Third, because mutual funds pay lower commissions to brokers, the expenses on transactions by funds indicate that, if anything, a greater turnover rate should be the norm in mutual funds as compared to investment accounts with similar objectives managed by brokers. Thus, there are reasons to believe that the turnover rates evidenced in mutual funds represent a respectable estimate of the level of turnover that professional managers regard as optimum.

As the above discussion indicates, trading activity inconsistent with that of mutual funds could usually be justified by a broker only if the customer's investment objectives differ from those of the funds, or if the broker had a realistic expectation of outperforming the mutual funds. Otherwise, the customer's funds might have been better placed with mutual funds.

In their discussion of mutual funds, the authors reference the *Morningstar Mutual Fund Sourcebook* that lists ten primary categories according to their investment objectives. Nine of the categories of interest represent a spectrum of goals. At one end of the investment objective continuum, aggressive growth funds offer increased returns with high risk. In contrast, an income fund's objective is steady, moderate income with lower risk.

Table 10.1 lists the fund types and turnover data for each type. The data indicate that there are real differences between the estimated optimum rates for diverse investment objectives.

Table 10.1: Fund Category and Turnover Statistics

| Category | Mean Turnover Rate | Std. Dev. | Mean Plus A Number Standard Deviations | | |
			1S.D.	2S.D.	3S.D.
Aggressive Growth (AG)	1.18	.72	1.90	2.62	3.35
Balanced (Bal)	.66	.58	1.23	1.81	2.38
Equity Income (EI)	.70	.53	1.23	1.76	2.29
Growth (G)	.98	.61	1.58	2.19	2.80
Growth-Income (GI)	.53	.55	1.09	1.64	2.19
International (Int)	.55	.42	.96	1.38	1.79
Option-Income (OI)	1.45	.74	2.19	2.93	3.67
Small Company (SC)	.54	.39	.93	1.32	1.71
Income (Inc)	.58	.40	.98	1.39	1.79

The majority of the differences in the mean turnover rates seen in Table 10.1 are statistically significant, which indicates that differences in the sample means are almost certainly not random occurrences and the optimal means for turnover rates apparently do vary between funds managed under distinctly different investment objectives. This conclusion is drawn from a computation of t-statistics for each possible pair of combinations as reported below in Table 10.2. More than half of the possible combinations show that turnover rates significantly differ between categories. From this, the authors contend that the categories have different optimal turnover rates. As an example, the mean turnover ratio for the aggressive growth funds shows significantly more turnover than does the mean for the balanced funds (t ratio = -7.20). The existence of significant differences between the sample means of the various categories of funds shows that the choice of investment objective influences the amount of turnover in funds handled by professional money managers.

Tables 10.1 and 10.2 show that the ratios for income, balanced, and growth-income funds, are all relatively low and not significantly different from each other. The authors posit that this is the case because managers of these funds generally invest in securities of mature firms. Interestingly, both international and small company funds also have low turnover ratios, even though these funds might be characterized as riskier or more speculative than many of the other categories. In the case of the small company funds, this may result from the long-term investment horizon required for the growth and maturation of small or start-up companies.

Table 10.2: T-Statistics

Cat.	AG	Bal	EI	G	GI	Int	OI	SC	Inc
AG		-7.2*	-6.89*	-2.84*	-9.3*	-9.47*	2.59*	-9.67*	-9.28*
Bal			.68	5.32*	-2.09*	-1.94	8.25*	-2.12*	-1.49
EI				4.82*	-2.93*	-2.84*	7.99*	-3.04*	-2.33*
G					-1.71	-7.96*	4.96*	-8.2*	-7.74*
GI						.31	9.78*	.14	1.01
Int							9.85*	-.19	.76
OI								-9.91*	-9.65*
SC									.98
Inc									

*significantly different at .05

It is seen that growth, aggressive growth, and option-income funds exhibit higher turnover ratios than any of the other fund categories. However, the highest turnover occurs in the option-income funds wherein managers generate cash flows by writing short-term call options against stocks held in the option-income funds' own portfolios.

The authors discuss that one can utilize this data to estimate what level of turnover activity may indicate excessive trading for accounts with corresponding investment goals. This is because the statistical likelihood of a turnover rate randomly exceeding the statistically approximated rate by more than two standard deviations is only 2.5%. For example, for the income fund category which has a sample mean of 0.58, a turnover ratio of 1.38 lies two standard deviations above the mean. They contend that it is unlikely that an income account invested in accordance with the funds' objective would exhibit a turnover rate at this high level.

The authors' next section entitled *Suggestions For Lower Benchmarks For Turnover Rates* ensues with an analysis of the disparity between the turnover rates characterizing mutual funds and those considered in many court cases to be excessive. In their survey of the relevant case law, it is seen that annual turnover ratios that seem fairly high by the findings of this study have been tolerated by the courts, often with some degree of confidence.

> In *Gleit v. Shearson, Hammill & Co.* the court stated that a turnover ratio of 2.97 seemed not excessive for an account with an investment goal of accumulating capital to defray children's college expenses. Another court, in *Van Alen v. Dominick & Dominick, Inc.*, stated that a turnover ratio of three was not excessive in the abstract or apparently for any investment objective and was further "not excessive in light of the [investor's] intent to 'build up' her account." The *Van Alen* court flatly stated that no court had found excessive trading based on an annual turnover ratio of three, plainly suggesting that such a rate was low. Yet another court, in *Grove v. Shearson Loeb Rhoades, Inc.*, concluded without significant comment that no excessive trading was indicated from the annual turnover ratio of 1.87 in light of the investor's goal of "increasing the return on her investment above the return on fixed income securities."[63]

---

[63] Winslow and Anderson, p. 353.

The authors explain that the broad-brush analysis used by the courts to bolster their holdings is unnecessary in light of their data. They discuss in several examples how the courts' determination of excess activity is often at substantial variance to the activity levels of appropriate mutual funds. Also, they give a brief history of how the *Harvard Law Review* Note's suggestion of six as a key figure became a guideline in many cases. The section ends on a cautionary note that prudence must be used in employing mutual fund activity rates as guides for activity rates in court determinations. They conclude the work with:

> At base, this Article indicates that courts should approach the analysis of excessive trading with a different attitude and that future decisions should move in a somewhat different direction from those currently on the books. Legal authorities suggest that significant deference has been given to the broker's judgment on this issue. The courts and commentators have failed to establish appropriate turnover rates (or ranges of rates) to be associated with diverse investment goals. Correction of these tendencies in line with the suggestions derived from our study of mutual fund data should improve significantly the use of turnover rates in the analysis of the excessive trading element of churning claims.[64]

---

[64] Winslow and Anderson, p. 361.

APPENDIX 10A: EXAMPLE OF A CHURNING CLAIM

In the paragraphs below, we give an overview of churning and excerpts from a churning claim filed as result of such improper account management. The underlying elements necessary for a churning claim to be pursued are examined in the next section. Section 10A.2 delineates the events which led to the filing of this particular churning claim. Section 10A.3 presents the highlights of an abbreviated Statement of Claim filed with the National Association of Securities Dealers (NASD). Case law references are footnoted.[65] The final section presents the outcome of the case.

10A.1 Elements of a Churning Claim

As broadly phrased over three decades ago, churning occurs "when a dealer, acting in his own interests and against those of his customer, induces transactions in the customer's account which are excessive in size and frequency in light of the character of the account."[66] This phrase belies the complex issues facing a customer who seeks a judgment against a broker for monetary damages. Three elements must be presented under a claim: "(1) 'control' over the account by the broker; (2) excessive trading in the account in light of the customer's objectives; and (3) scienter,

---

[65] The author references a single secondary source (see footnote 2) owing to space considerations.

[66] See Donald A. Winslow and Seth C. Anderson, "A Model for Determining the Excessive Trading Element in a Churning Claim." *North Carolina Law Review*, Vol. 68, No.2, January 1990, Fn. No. 1, p. 327.

an intent to defraud or a reckless disregard for the customer's best interest by the broker. The apparent clarity of this statement of the churning elements masks the difficulty of determining the existence of churning in a particular case. Each of the three elements possesses a degree of analytical difficulty."[67]

The first issue to be proven, that of control, can occur in two ways: (1) customer-granted discretion over account activity, and (2) indirect control results from an unsophisticated investor's reliance on the broker's expertise and assumed honesty. Excessive trading is the second element of a churning claim and for years was considered to be the "most difficult for plaintiffs to establish and the most troublesome for courts to evaluate."[68] However, in 1967 Goldberg proposed a 2-4-6 Rule, which because of its simplicity gained popularity for determining excessive trading. According to this rule, an annualized turnover ratio of two times the average equity in an account is presumed acceptable. An annualized turnover rate of four is cause for suspicion, and a rate of six presumes churning.[69] Recently, a more theoretically justified model was developed by Winslow and Anderson (1990) wherein mutual fund turnover ratios proxy appropriate turnover rates for portfolios with differing objectives. Their model offers turnover ratios in the 1.5 to 2.5 range as indicative of excessive trading.[70] Often tied to the excessive trading element in churning claims are both the expense ratio and the average-period held statistic. Scienter, is the third element of a churning claim, is a reckless

---

[67] Ibid. Fn. No. 3 @ p. 328.

[68] Ibid. Fn. No. 4 @ p. 328.

[69] Ibid. Fn. No. 58 @ p. 339.

[70] Ibid. pp. 350-352.

disregard of the customer's best interests and can take various forms, including: misappropriation of client funds, unauthorized transactions, and unsuitable securities, among others.   Now that we have covered the underlying issues of a churning claim, the next section presents a brief review of the facts involved in an actual churning claim.

10A.2 Background of a Churning Claim

Mrs. Cope is a 67-year old widow who lives in Anytown, Anystate. Her educational level is high school graduate with no business experience.   Her late husband handled all financial matters, even the checking account, and she never had experience in this area. After his death, her assets consisted of $60,000 in certificates of deposit (CDs), $90,000 of life insurance proceeds to be paid in the near future, and a $90,000 mortgage-free house. Social Security provided her primary income.

In late February, 1996, Mrs. Cope contacted Big Investments about an investment for which she had been solicited by a brokerage firm in New York. The New York firm had pitched her about an insurance company stock, and she decided to contact Big Investments because she attended church with Manager Jones at their Anytown branch office. Mr. Jones was not available, but her call was transferred to Broker Smith, a registered representative at the firm. Mrs. Cope asked Mr. Smith about the insurance stock. Mr. Smith told Mrs. Cope that he invested money for his grandmother (whom Mrs. Cope also knew) and convinced her to open an account with him. She told him that she had $60,000 in maturing CDs with which she wished to get a larger, safe return. Over the following months Mrs. Cope became quite comfortable with this polite young man. In late spring of 1996, Mrs. Cope decided to invest the insurance monies of $90,000 and asked Smith to invest it safely.   Around March of 1997, Mrs. Cope decided to withdraw $29,000 in order to help her son with a financial need and learned that her original $150,000 was worth only $23,790. Mrs. Cope got extremely upset and wrote a letter to Manager Jones telling him of her dissatisfaction, but Jones failed to return several calls made by Mrs. Cope.

Mrs. Cope confided in her son, who convinced her to get a lawyer. The lawyer contacted an expert witness, who discovered an annual turnover ratio of 15.5 and commissions/margin expense, totaling $60,730. At the lawyer's request, the expert computed the amount that Mrs. Cope's account should have been worth under two scenarios: (1) investing in CDs, and (2) investing in an equity index such as the Dow Jones Industrial Average. As a result, the initial loss computations in Mrs. Cope's account at Big Investments were $135,210 and $158,379, respectively. These amounts would be utilized along with other expenses allowed by law to arrive at a final damages amount of $202,540.

10A.3 Statement of Claim Filed with the NASD

Helen P.Cope asked that we write this Statement of Claim on her behalf requesting arbitration of disputes arising out of the handling of Mrs. Cope's account by Big Investments and its registered representative, Broker Smith, hereinafter collectively referred to as "Respondents."

Summary of Claim

From February, 1996, through April, 1997, Helen P.Cope maintained an account at Big Investments. Her broker was Broker Smith. As a result of the improper and fraudulent manner in which the Respondents handled Mrs. Cope's account, she sustained damages and is seeking recovery of her damages in excess of $202,540. The improper and fraudulent conduct of the Respondents includes:

(a)   excessive trading;
(b)   directing and effecting unsuitable trades in Mrs. Cope's account; and
(c)   misrepresentation of risks associated with the investments sold to Mrs. Cope.

In the handling of Mrs. Cope's account, the Respondents' actions constitute breach of contract, failure to supervise, negligent misrepresentation, breach of fiduciary duty, violations of state securities laws, and violations of the rules of the National Association of Securities Dealers, Inc. (NASD), and the New York Stock Exchange, Inc. (NYSE).

Background Facts

The background facts presented in this section of the claim were delineated in the above section "Background of a Churning Claim." The primary conclusion of this section is that Mrs. Cope was never in a position to put her money into risky investments.

10A.4 Analysis and Authorities

The facts herein establish that Mrs. Cope's account was churned by the Respondents and that various unauthorized trades were made. Stock purchases were made on margin without disclosure of the inherent risks and increased costs of such a practice. Respondents recommended many investments that were unsuitable for her account. The only parties who benefitted from these practices were Respondents, who received thousands of dollars in commissions and other fees. Mrs. Cope, on the other hand, suffered damages in excess of $202,540 as a result of Respondents' egregious conduct. Respondent, Big Investments, is liable for the conduct of its employees under general agency law principles as a control person, as an aider and abettor, and by reason of its inadequate supervision of Smith.

Breach of Duty and Breach of Contract

As the facts illustrate, the Respondents clearly breached their contractual obligations to Claimant and breached the duties they owed Mrs. Cope in connection with the handling of her account. The NASD and NYSE rules "set out general standards of industry conduct" and are evidence of the standard of care to which broker dealers must abide in the handling of their clients' accounts.[71] By their conduct as outlined above, Respondents failed to abide by the rules as set out in the NASD and NYSE, including the following:

(1)   Rule 2110 of the NASD Conduct Rules and Rule 401 of the NYSE (members will observe high standards of commercial honor and just and equitable principles of trade);

(2)   Rules 2310 and 3010 of the NASD Conduct Rules and Rule 405(1) of the NYSE (suitability and know your customer rules),

(3)   Rule 2310-2(b)(2) of the NASD Conduct Rules (prohibition of excessive trading);

(4)   Rule 2120 of the NASD Conduct Rules (prohibition of the use of any manipulative, deceptive or other fraudulent device or contrivance); and,

---

[71] Ibid., No. 16, p. 330.

(5)   Rule 3010 of the NASD Conduct Rules and Rule 405(2) of the NYSE (duty to supervise).

By churning Mrs. Cope's account, purchasing stocks on margin absent permission, and purchasing unsuitable investments, Respondents failed to abide by these industry rules and are liable to Mrs. Cope for their negligence. By violating the NASD Conduct Rules, Respondents repeatedly breached this contractual duty, causing Mrs. Cope damages in excess of $202,540.

Churning and Excessive Trading

Respondents directed excessive trades in Claimant's account and otherwise churned Claimant's account. The elements of the claim are as follows:

(1)   The trading in the accounts was excessive in light of the client's investment objectives;

(2)   The broker controlled the accounts either through formal discretion, unauthorized trading, or by having the client routinely accept his recommendations; and

(3)   The broker acted with intent to defraud or with willful or reckless disregard for the client's interest.

The first of these elements is proven in this case by application of the three main mathematical tests for excessive trading which are followed by the SEC and the courts.

First, the annual turnover rate is a measure frequently relied upon by courts in a claim for churning. During the period Broker Smith was handling Mrs. Cope's account, the annual turnover rate was 15.5. This rate is clearly excessive in light of Mrs. Cope's investment goals.

The second mathematical test used to determine the excessiveness of trading is the cost-equity ratio. The cost-equity ratio is the same as the rate of return an account would have to earn just to pay commissions, margin interest, and fees, without earning any profit for the account. The cost-equity ratio in Mrs. Cope's account was an obscene 102% on an annualized basis.

The third mathematical test used to determine if there is churning in an account is the length of time that stocks were held in Mrs. Cope account prior to their sale or transfer. In Mrs. Cope's account, 81% of the positions were held for 90 or fewer days, and 69% of the positions were held for less than 60 days. Approximately 47% of the positions in Mrs. Cope's account were held for 30 days or less. This certainly indicates excessive trading. The excessiveness of the trading that Respondents conducted with the funds in Mrs. Cope's account satisfies the first element of Mrs. Cope's churning claim against Respondents. The second requirement for establishing a churning claim is the broker's control over the trading in question. Respondents clearly controlled the trading in Mrs. Cope's account. Mrs. Cope trusted Respondents to handle her account, since she lacked the knowledge to do so. Finally, there can be no doubt that the Respondents, who profited from commission and margin interest, acted willfully or at a minimum, with careless and reckless indifference to Mrs. Cope. Her loss was very much their gain; hence scienter existed.

Suitability

As previously noted, Respondents directed transactions in Claimant's account and generally handled Claimant's account in a patently unsuitable manner. Respondents were aware that Mrs. Cope did not intend to risk her money to generate large commissions or to purchase securities on margin. The unsuitable trading in Mrs. Cope's account violated many of the various laws, rules and regulations set out above, resulting in damages to Mrs. Cope in excess of $202,540.

Failure to Supervise

Pursuant to Rule 3010 of the NASD Conduct Rules and 405(2) of the NYSE Rules, Big Investments had a duty to diligently supervise the activities of its agent, Broker Smith, in handling Mrs. Cope's account. Big Investments failed to detect, or wrongfully permitted, the excessive and inappropriate trading which occurred in Mrs. Cope's account. Big Investments is liable, therefore, to Mrs. Cope for its failure to adequately supervise Broker Smith regarding his handling of Mrs. Cope's account.

Fraud/Negligent Misrepresentation

In recommending and effecting purchases in Mrs. Cope's account, Respondents engaged in fraudulent practices and knowingly, recklessly, and intentionally, made numerous omissions of material facts. Respondents never apprised Claimant of the risks involved with the investments they purchased and sold in her account. Respondents' omissions are a violation of both Anystate common law and statutory prohibition.

Breach of Fiduciary Duty

A securities broker is a fiduciary of the client. Specifically, the Eleventh Circuit Court of Appeals has identified the fiduciary responsibilities of a broker to include the following:

> (1)   To recommend a stock only after studying it sufficiently to become informed as to its nature,

price, and financial prognosis;

(2)   To carry out the customer's orders promptly in the manner best suited to serve the customer's interests;

(3)   To inform the customer of the risks involved in purchases or selling a particular security;

(4)   To refrain from self-dealing...;

(5)   Not to misrepresent any fact material to the transaction; and

(6)   To transact business only after receiving prior authorization from the customer.

By violating these duties, as well as the NASD and NYSE rules governing excessive trading, unauthorized trading, suitability, supervision, and other rules designed to protect customers, Respondents have breached the fiduciary duties they owed to Mrs. Cope, causing her damages in excess of $202,540.

10A.5 Damages

Under current precedent in the Eleventh Circuit, a customer whose account is churned is entitled to recover: (1) both the commissions and other fees paid, and (2) the benefits that a well-managed portfolio would have brought the client.

Commissions and Other Fees Paid

According to *Miley*, when a customer's account has been churned, the brokerage firm must reimburse commissions and other charges (including margin interest) regardless of whether the investor's portfolio increased or decreased as a result of any of the trades.[72] Claimant is able to ascertain that she was charged at least

---

[72] Ibid., Fn. No. 16, p. 330.

$52,370 in total commissions for her account and $8,360 in margin interest during the period that Smith handled her account.

The Benefits of a Well-Managed Portfolio

A well-managed portfolio would have been worth at least $141,810 more than Claimant's account was worth when Claimant's account was transferred to another Representative. In other words, using the Dow Jones Industrial Averages ("the Dow"), had Claimant's account performed like the Dow from the time she opened her account in late February, 1996, Claimant's original $60,000 would have earned 21% simply as a result of increases in the Dow. Mrs. Cope's account did not merely underperform the Dow during this time frame; instead, she actually lost money in her account as a result of Respondents' improper and fraudulent practices. Additionally, had the $90,000 that was deposited in the account in late spring, 1996, been invested in a safe, income-producing instrument as she requested, these funds would have been worth $93,000 on April 30, 1997, assuming a conservative estimated return of 5%. Applicable state law also entitles Claimant to recover her losses, lost profits, and the commissions she paid. Had Respondents fully performed their contract with her, Mrs. Cope would have at least $141,810 more than she has today.

Punitive Damages

Mrs. Cope also is entitled to punitive damages for the offensive conduct perpetrated by the Respondents. The *Miley* court indicated that an award of punitive damages equal to three times the compensatory damage is reasonable in a churning case.

Attorneys' Fees

Under Sec. 8-6-19 of the Anystate Securities Act, attorneys' fees also may be recovered if Respondents have violated the provisions of the Anystate Securities Act. As a result of Respondents' action, Claimant has had to pursue this arbitration to recover the damages to which she is entitled. As such, Respondents should be held responsible for the costs of this action to include attorneys' fees as provided for under the Act.

10A.6 Demand for Relief

Based upon the foregoing, Mrs. Cope demands judgment against Big Investments as follows:

(A)   for the reimbursement of all the commissions, believed to be in excess of $52,370 charged against Mrs. Cope's account;

(B)   for the reimbursement of all margin interest, believed to be in excess of $8,360 charged against Mrs. Cope's account;

(C)   for a loss of $141,810 representing the difference in performance between Mrs. Cope's account and a well-managed account;

(D)   for punitive damages in an amount to be determined by the arbitrator in the exercise of his or her discretion, such damages being awarded to punish Respondents for their wrongful conduct and to deter such conduct in the future;

(E)   for all of Mrs. Cope's costs, expenses, and disbursements, including attorneys' fees, associated with this arbitration proceeding. An award of

attorneys' fees is permitted under the Anystate
Securities Act; Code of §8-6-19; and

(F)   for such other relief as the arbitrator deems just and
proper.

10A.7 Demand for Arbitration

Based upon the foregoing, Mrs. Cope requests arbitration of
her disputes with Big Investments and Broker Smith before a
single arbitrator in Washington, D.C., acting under sponsorship of
the National Association of Securities Dealers, Inc.

Respectfully submitted,
Attorney for Helen P.Cope

10A.8 Outcome

The Statement of Claim was filed with the NASD and copied
to the State Securities Commission. Several months later, Big
Investments' attorneys made a settlement offer of $50,000, but that
was immediately refused. Two subsequent offers of $80,000 and
$100,000 were refused. During this time, the State Securities
Commission discovered that several other suits were pending
against this same branch office and began the initial stages of a
formal investigation. Shortly thereafter, the plaintiff accepted an
offer of $200,000 for settlement.

XI: CONCLUSION

The purpose of this book is to make readily accessible a broad overview of the investment arena facing both individual and professional investment managers. Initially, the investment process itself is outlined, and this is followed by a brief depiction of the historical backdrop for today's investment environment in which both active and passive players participate.

The two basic schools of thought, the efficient market theorists and the traditionalists, are briefly discussed in Chapter IV. Following that, the efficacy of analysts' recommendations is considered in Chapter V. How well investors fare via the services of professional managers is revealed in Chapter VI. The findings of the studies therein which investigate mutual fund performance are somewhat sobering, as it is evident that most investors employing equity mutual funds receive little other than a choice of fund objectives, record-keeping, and diversification, in return for the costs they incur. However, these same services are readily available from much lower cost index funds.

Equally as sobering are the findings of individual investor studies in Chapter VII, which show that, on average, investors tend to make ineffectual buy and sell decisions and often pay substantial commissions in the process of doing so. To assess the impact of both professional and individual management costs, Chapter VIII presents the impact of these costs in an historical return perspective. As is seen in Chapter VIII, investment costs can essentially reduce profits from mutual funds by up to 33% on average over a 15-year period, and even more so for mutual funds with loads. Also, in this chapter it is seen that investors who trade an average amount at discount or full-service brokers over a typical 15-year period generate costs which reduce their net profits by approximately 28% and 47%, respectively. As to whether these investor profit forfeitures are reasonable or are evidence of mismanagement, is for the reader to decide.

To facilitate the reader's assessment of appropriate management versus mismanagement, the last two chapters address the constructs of suitability and of churning. Chapter IX comprises a summary of "Defining Suitability" which presents suitability in a modern portfolio theory perspective. Chapter X first focuses primarily on an early article which essentially defines and discusses churning and, second, on a later work which presents economically justifiable guidelines for assessing excessive trading activity in an investment account.

REFERENCES

Abarbanell, J., 1991, "Do Analysts' Earnings Forecasts Incorporate Information in Prior Stock Price Changes?," *Journal of Accounting and Economics*, 14, 147-166.

Abarbanell, J. and V. Bernard, 1992, "Analysts' Overreaction/Underreaction to Earnings Information as an Explanation for Anomalous Stock Price Behavior," *The Journal of Finance*, 47, 1181-1207.

Anderson, S., 1986, "Closed-end Funds versus Market Efficiency," *The Journal of Portfolio Management*, 13, 63-65.

Anderson, S., 1989, "Evidence on the Reflecting Barriers Model: New Opportunities for Technical Analysis?," *Financial Analysts Journal*, 45, 67-71.

Anderson, S., 1992, "A 'Free Market' Response to Cochrane et al. and the Status Quo," *The Journal of Corporation Law*, 18, 91-99.

Anderson, S. and P. Ahmed, 2005, *Mutual Funds: Fifty Years of Research Findings*, Boston: Springer Publishers.

Anderson, S., and J. Born, 1992, *Closed-End Investment Companies: Issues and Answers*, Boston: Kluwer Academic Publishers.

Anderson, S. and J. Born, 2002, *Closed-end Fund Pricing: Theories and Evidence*, Boston: Kluwer Academic Publishers.

Anderson, S., B. Coleman, and J. Born, 2001, "A Closer Look at Trading Strategies for U.S. Equity Closed-end Investment Companies," *Financial Services Review*, 10, 237-248.

Anderson, S. and O. Schnusenberg, 2005, "A Review of Studies in Mutual Fund Performance, Timing, and Persistence," Working Paper, University of North Florida.

Anderson, S. and H. Stranahan, 2005, "Account Turnover Based on Demographic Profiles: Which Investors Trade Too Much?," Working Paper, University of North Florida.

Anderson, S. and D. Winslow, 1992, "Defining Suitability," *Kentucky Law Journal*, 81, 105-122.

Asness, C., 1995, "The Power of Past Stock Returns to Explain Future Stock Returns," Working paper, University of Chicago.

Badrinath, S. and W. Lewellen, 1991, "Evidence on Tax-Motivated Securities Trading Behavior," *The Journal of Finance*, 66, 369-382.

Baks, K., A. Metrick, and J. Wachter, 2001, "Should Investors Avoid All Actively Managed Mutual Funds? A Study in Bayesian Performance Evaluation," *The Journal of Finance*, 56, 45-85.

Ball, R., S. Kothari, and J. Shanken, 1995, "Problems in Measuring Portfolio Performance: An Application to Contrarian Investment Strategies," *Journal of Financial Economics*, 38, 79-107.

Barber, B., R. Lehavy, M. McNichols, and B. Trueman, 2001, "Can Investors Profit from the Prophets? Security Analyst Recommendations and Stock Returns," The Journal of Finance, 56, 531-563.

Barber, B., R. Lehavy, M. McNichols, and B. Trueman, 2003, "Prophets and Losses: Reassessing the Returns to Analysts' Recommendations," *Financial Analyst Journal*, 59, 88-96.

Barber, B. and D. Loeffler, 1993, "The 'Dartboard' Column: Second-Hand Information and Price Pressure," *Journal of Financial and Quantitative Analysis*, 28, 273-284.

Barber, B. and T. Odean, 2000a, "Trading Is Hazardous to Your Wealth: the Common Stock Investment Performance of Individual Investors," *The Journal of Finance* 52, 773-806.

Barber, B. and T. Odean, 2000b, "Too Many Cooks Spoil the Profits: Investment Club Performance," *Financial Analyst Journal*, January/February, 17-25.

Barber, B. and T. Odean, 2001, "Boys Will Be Boys: Gender, Overconfidence, and Common Stock Investment," *Quarterly Journal of Economics*, February, 261-292.

Bauer, R., K. Koedijk, and R. Otten, 2005, "International Evidence on Ethical Mutual Fund Performance and Investment Style," *Journal of Banking & Finance*, 29, 1751-1767.

Becker, C., W. Ferson, D. Myers, and M. Schill, 1999, "Conditional Market Timing with Benchmark Investors," *Journal of Financial Economics,* 52, 119-148.

Benesh, G. and S. Perfect, 1997, "An Analysis of *Value Line*'s Ability to Forecast Long-Run Returns," *Journal of Financial and Strategic Decisions*, 10, 1-10.

Berk, J. and R. Green, 2004, "Mutual Fund Flows and Performance in Rational Markets," *Journal of Political Economy*, 112, 1269-1295.

Bernard, V. and J. Thomas, 1989, "Post-Earnings-Announcement Drift: Delayed Price Response or Risk Premium?," *Journal of Accounting Research, Supplement*, 27, 1 - 48.

Bernard, V. and J. Thomas, 1990, "Evidence that Stock Prices Do Not Fully Reflect the Implications of Current Earnings for Future Earnings," *Journal of Accounting and Economics*, 13, 305-340.

Bers, M. and J. Madura, 2000, "The Performance Persistence of Closed-End Funds," *Financial Review*, 35, 33-52.

Bessembinder, H., 2003, "Issues in Assessing Trade Execution Costs," *Journal of Financial Markets*, 6, 235-258.

Bjerring, J. H., J. Lakonishok, and T.Vermaelen, 1983, "Stock Prices and Financial Analysts' Recommendations," *The Journal of Finance* 38, 187-204.

Black, F., 1973, "Yes, Virginia, There Is Hope: Tests of the *Value Line* Ranking System," *Financial Analysts Journal*, 29, 10-14.

Black, F., 1986, "Noise," *The Journal of Finance*, 41, 529-543.

Bliss, R. and M. Potter, 2002, "Mutual Fund Managers: Does Gender Matter?," *Journal of Business and Economic Studies*, 8, 1-17.

Blume, M., J. Crockett, and I. Friend, 1974, "Stock Ownership in the United States: Characteristics and Trends," *Survey of Current Business*, November, 16-40.

Bogle, J., 2005, "The Mutual Fund Industry 60 Years Later: For Better or Worse?," *Financial Analysts Journal*, Jan./Feb.,15-24.

Bollen, N. and J. Busse, 2001, "On the Timing Ability of Mutual Fund Managers," *The Journal of Finance*, 56, 1075-1094.

Branch, B., 1977, "A Tax Loss Trading Rule," *Journal of Business*, 50, 198-207.

Brandeis, L., 1914, *Other People's Money and How the Bankers Use It*, Reprint, New York: Augustus M. Kelley, 1971.

Brown, S. and W. Goetzmann, 1995, "Performance Persistence," *The Journal of Finance*, 50, 679-698.

Brown, S. and P. Pope, 1996, "Post-Earnings Announcement Drift?," Working paper, New York University.

Brown, F. and D. Vickers, 1963, "Mutual Fund Portfolio Activity, Performance, and Market Impact," *The Journal of Finance*, 18, 377-391.

Campbell, J. and J. Cochrane, 1994, "By Force of Habit: A Consumption Based Explanation of Aggregate Stock Market Behavior," Working paper, University of Chicago.

Cantwell, E., D. Chambers, and J. Zdanowicz, 1988, "Stockbroker – Customer Disputes: Churning Spurs Litigation," *Trial*, 24, 46-55.

Carhart, M., 1997, "On Persistence in Mutual Fund Performance," *The Journal of Finance*, 52, 57-82.

Carlson, R., 1970, "Aggregate Performance of Mutual Funds, 1948-1967," *Journal of Financial and Quantitative Analysis*, 5, 1-32.

Carmel, J. and M. Young, 1997, "Long Horizon Mean Reversion in the Stock Market: The Postwar Years," Working paper, University of Michigan Business School.

Chan, K., 1986, "Can Tax-Loss Selling Explain the January Seasonality in Stock Returns?," *The Journal of Finance*, 41, 1115-1128.

Chan, L., H. Chen, and J. Lakonishok, 2002, "On Mutual Fund Investment Styles," *Review of Financial Studies*, 15, 1407-1437.

Chan, L., N. Jegadeesh, and J. Lakonishok, 1996, "Momentum Strategies," *The Journal of Finance*, 51, 1681-1714.

Chang, E. and W. Lewellen, 1984, "Market Timing and Mutual Fund Investment Performance," *The Journal of Business,* 57, 57-72.

Chen, J., H. Hong, M. Huang, and J. Kubik, 2004, "Does Fund Size Erode Mutual Fund Performance? The Role of Liquidity and Organization," *American Economic Review*, 94, 1276-1302.

Chopra, N., J. Lakonishok, and J. Ritter, 1992, "Measuring Abnormal Performance: Do Stocks Overreact?," *Journal of Financial Economics*, 31, 235-268.

"Churning by Securities Dealers," 1968, *Harvard Law Review* Note.

Close, J., 1952, "Investment Companies: Closed-End versus Open-End," *Harvard Business Review*, 29, 79-88.

Cohen, R., J. Coval, and L. Pastor, 2004, "Judging Fund Managers by the Company They Keep," *The Journal of Finance*, 60, 1057.

Cohn, R., W. Lewellen, R. Lease, and G. Schlarbaum, 1975, "Individual Investor Risk Aversion and Investment Portfolio Composition," *The Journal of Finance*, 30, 605-620.

Constantinides, G., 1984, "Optimal Stock Trading With Personal Taxes," *Journal of Financial Economics*, 13, 65-89.

Copeland, T. and D. Mayers, 1982, "The *Value Line* Enigma (1965- 1978): A Case Study of Performance Evaluation Issues," *Journal of Financial Economics*, 10, 289-322.

Cowles 3rd, A., 1933, "Can Stock Market Forecasters Forecast?," *Econometrica*, 3, 309- 324.

Daniel, K., 1996, "The Power and Size of Asset Pricing Tests," Working paper, University of Chicago.

Daniel, K., D. Hirshleifer, and A. Subrahmanyam, 1998, "Investor Psychology and Security Market Under- and Overreactions," *The Journal of Finance*, 53, 1839- 1866.

Davies, P. and M. Canes, 1978, "Stock Prices and the Publication of Second-Hand Information," *Journal of Business*, 51, 43-56.

DeBondt, W. and R. Thaler, 1985, "Does the Stock Market Overreact?," *The Journal of Finance*, 40, 793 - 808.

DeBondt, W. and R. Thaler, 1987, "Further Evidence on Investor Overreaction and Stock Market Seasonality," *The Journal of Finance*, 42, 557-581.

Dechow, P. and R. Sloan, 1997, "Returns to Contrarian Investment Strategies: Tests of Naive Expectations Hypotheses," *Journal of Financial Economics*, 41, 3-27.

Dellva, W. and G. Olson, 1998, "The Relationship Between Mutual Fund Fees and Expenses and Their Effects on Performance," *The Financial Review*, 33, 85-104.

Desai, H. and P. Jain, 1997, "Long-Run Common Stock Returns Following Stock Splits and Reverse Splits Dividends," *Journal of Business*, 70, 409-434.

Dharan, B. and D. Ikenberry, 1995, "The Long-Run Negative Drift of Post-Listing Stock Returns," *The Journal of Finance*, 50, 1547-1574.

diBartolomeo, D. and E. Witkowski, 1997, "Mutual Fund Misclassification: Evidence Based on Style Analysis," *Financial Analysts Journal*, Sept/Oct, 32-43.

Dickson, J., J. Shoven, and C. Sialm, 2000, "Tax Externalities of Equity Mutual Funds," *National Tax Journal*, 53, 607-628.

Dimson, E. and P. Marsh, 1984, "An Analysis of Brokers' and Analysts' Unpublished Forecasts of UK Stock Returns," *The Journal of Finance*, 39, 1257-1292.

Douglas, W., 1940, *Democracy and Finance*, Kennikat Press.

Dyl, E., 1977, "Capital Gains, Taxation, and Year-End Stock Market Behavior," *The Journal of Finance*, 32, 165-175.

Elton, E., M. Gruber, and C. Blake, 2003, "Incentive Fees and Mutual Funds," *The Journal of Finance*, 58, 779-804.

Elton, E., M. Gruber, and S. Grossman, 1986, "Discrete Expectational Data and Portfolio Performance," *The Journal of Finance*, 41, 699-712.

Elton, E., M. Gruber, and M. Gultekin, 1984, "Professional Expectations: Accuracy and Diagnosis of Errors," *Journal of Financial and Quantitative Analysis*, 19, 351-363.

Fama, E., 1998, "Market Efficiency, Long-Term Returns and Behavioral Finance," *Journal of Financial Economics*, 49, 283-306.

Fama, E. and K. French, 1988, "Permanent and Temporary Components of Stock Prices," *Journal of Political Economy* 96, 246-273.

Fama, E. and K. French, 1993, "Common Risk Factors in the Returns on Stocks and Bonds," *Journal of Financial Economics*, 33, 3-56.

Fama, E. and K. French, 1996, "Multifactor Explanations of Asset Pricing Anomalies," *The Journal of Finance*, 51, 55-84.

FBI Website, accessed January, 2004, http://www.fbi.gov.

Feldman, A., 2001, "Sue Your Broker", *Money*, October, 102-110.

Ferson, W. and R. Schadt, 1996, "Measuring Fund Strategy and Performance in Changing Economic Conditions," *The Journal of Finance,* 51, 425-461.

Ferson, W. and V. Warther, 1996, "Evaluating Fund Performance in a Dynamic Market," *Financial Analysts Journal*, 52, 20-28.

Gaspar, J., M. Massa, and P. Matos, 2005, "Favoritism in Mutual Fund Families? Evidence on Strategic Cross-Fund Subsidization," *The Journal of Finance*, 61, 73.

Goetzmann, W. and R. Ibbotson, 1994, "Do Winners Repeat? Patterns in Mutual Fund Return Behavior," *The Journal of Portfolio Management,* Winter, 9-18.

Goldberg, S., 1978, *Fraudulent Broker-Dealer Practices*, American Institute for Securities Regulation.

Gompers, P. and J. Lerner, 1998, "Venture Capital Distributions: Short-Run and Long-Run Reactions," *The Journal of Finance*, 53, 2161-2183.

Gordon v. New York Stock Exchange, 422 U.S. 659(1975) Case Number: 74-304.

Grant, D., 1977, "Portfolio Performance and the 'Cost' of Timing Decisions," *The Journal of Finance*, 32, 837-846.

Grinblatt, M., R. Masulis, and S. Titman, 1984, "The Valuation Effects of Stock Splits and Stock Dividends," *Journal of Financial Economics*, 13, 97-112.

Grinblatt, M. and S. Titman, 1989, "Mutual Fund Performance: an Analysis of Quarterly Portfolio Holdings," *The Journal of Business*, 62, 393-416.

Grinblatt, M. and S. Titman, 1993, "Performance Measurement without Benchmarks: An Examination of Mutual Fund Returns," *The Journal of Business*, 66, 47-68.

Grossman, S., 1975, "Essays on Rational Expectations," Unpublished Doctoral Dissertation, University of Chicago.

Grossman, S., 1976, "On the Efficiency of Competitive Stock Markets Where Traders Have Diverse Information," *The Journal of Finance*, 31, 573-585.

Grossman, S., 1978, "Further Results on the Informational Efficiency of Competitive Stock Markets," *Journal of Economic Theory*, 18, 81-101.

Grossman, S. and J. Stiglitz, 1980, "On the Impossibility of Informationally Efficient Markets," *American Economic Review*, 70, 393-409.

Groth, J., W. Lewellen, G. Scharlbaum, and R. Lease, 1979, "An Analysis of Brokerage House Securities Recommendations," *Financial Analysts Journal*, 35, 32-40.

Gruber, M., 1996, "Another Puzzle: The Growth in Actively Managed Mutual Funds," *The Journal of Finance*, 51, 783-810.

Haugen, R. and N. Baker, 1996, "Commonality in the Determinants of Expected Stock Returns," *Journal of Financial Economics*, 41, 401-439.

Hendricks, D., J. Patel, and R. Zeckhauser, 1993, "Hot Hands in Mutual Funds: Short-run Persistence of Relative Performance, 1974-1988," *The Journal of Finance*, 43, 93-130.

Hendricks, D., J. Patel, and R. Zeckhauser, 1997, "The J-shape of Performance Persistence Given Survivorship Bias," *Review of Economics and Statistics*, 79, 161-166.

Henriksson, R. and R. Merton, 1981, "On Market Timing and Investment Performance," *The Journal of Business*, 54, 513-533.

Herman, E., 1963, "Mutual Fund Management Fee Rates," *The Journal of Finance*, 18, 360-376.

Holloway, C., 1981, "A Note on Testing Aggressive Investment Strategy Using *Value Line* Ranks," *The Journal of Finance*, 36, 711-719.

Ibbotson Associates, 2002, *Stocks, Bonds, Bills, and Inflation: 2002 Yearbook*, Chicago: Ibbotson Associates.

Ikenberry, D., J. Lakonishok, and T. Vermaelen, 1995, "Market Underreaction to Open Market Share Repurchases," *Journal of Financial Economics*, 39, 181-208.

Ikenberry, D., G. Rankine, and E. K. Stice, 1996, "What Do Stock Splits Really Signal?," *Journal of Financial and Quantitative Analysis*, 31, 357-375.

Indro, D., C. Jiang, M. Hu, and W. Lee, 1999, "Mutual Fund Performance: Does Size Matter?," *Financial Analysts Journal*, 55, 74-87.

Jagannathan, R. and R. Korajczyk, 1986, "Assessing the Market Timing Performance of Managed Portfolios," *The Journal of Business*, 59, 217-235.

Jain, P. and J. Wu, 2000, "Truth in Mutual Fund Advertising: Evidence on Future Performance and Fund Flows," *The Journal of Finance*, 55, 937-958.

Jegadeesh, N., 1990, "Evidence of Predictable Behavior of Security Returns," *The Journal of Finance*, 45, 881-898.

Jegadeesh, N. and S. Titman, 1993, "Returns to Buying Winners and Selling Losers: Implications for Stock Market Efficiency," *The Journal of Finance*, 48, 65-91.

Jennings, R. and H. Marsh, Jr., 1987, *Securities Regulation, 6th ed.*, 558-559, New York: The Foundation Press.

Jensen, M., 1968, "The Performance of Mutual Funds in the Period 1945-1964," *The Journal of Finance,* 23, 389-416.

Jiang, W., 2003, "A Nonparametric Test of Market Timing," *Journal of Empirical Finance*, 10, 399-425.

Jones, C., R. Rendleman, Jr., and H. Latané, 1985, "Earnings Announcements: Pre-And-Post Responses," *Journal of Portfolio Management*, 11, 28-33.

Joy, O., R. Litzenberger, and R. McEnally, 1977, "The Adjustment of Stock Prices to Announcements of Unanticipated Changes in Quarterly Earnings," *Journal of Accounting Research*, 15, 207-225.

Kahn, R. and A. Rudd, 1995, "Does Historical Performance Predict Future Performance?," *Financial Analysts Journal*, 51, 43-52.

Kahneman, D. and A. Tversky, 1979, "Prospect Theory: An Analysis of Decision Under Risk," *Econometrica*, 46, 171-185.

Kang, J., Y. Kim, and R. Stulz, 1996, "The Underreaction Hypothesis and the New Issue Puzzle: Evidence from Japan," *Review of Financial Studies*, 12, 519-534.

Kaul, G. and M. Nimalendran, 1990, "Price Reversals: Bid-Ask Errors or Market Overreaction?," *Journal of Financial Economics*, 28, 67-93.

Kihlstrom, R. and L. Mirman, 1975, "Information and Market Equilibrium," *Journal of Economics*, 6, 357-376.

Kim, M., C. Nelson, and R. Startz, 1988, "Mean Reversion in Stock Prices? A Reappraisal of the Empirical Evidence," *Review of Economic Studies*, 58, 551-528.

Kleidon, A., 1986, "Bias in Small Sample Tests of Stock Price Rationality," *Journal of Business*, 59, 237-261.

Kon, S., 1983, "The Market-Timing Performance of Mutual Fund Managers," *The Journal of Business*, 56, 323-347.

Kon, S. and F. Jen, 1979, "The Investment Performance of Mutual Funds: An Empirical Investigation of Timing, Selectivity and Market Efficiency," *The Journal of Business*, 52, 263-289.

Kothari, S. and J. Warner, 2001, "Evaluating Mutual Fund Performance," *The Journal of Finance*, 56, 1985-2010.

Krooss, H. and M. Blyn, 1971, *A History of Financial Intermediaries*, New York: Random House.

Lakonishok, J., A. Shleifer, and R. Vishny, 1992, "The Structure and Performance of the Money Management Industry," *Brookings Papers on Economic Activity*, Vol., 339-391.

Lakonishok, J., A. Shleifer, and R. Vishny, 1994, "Contrarian Investment, Extrapolation and Risk," *The Journal of Finance*, 49, 1541-1578.

Lakonishok, J. and T. Vermaelen, 1990, "Anomalous Price Behavior Around Repurchase Tender Offers," *The Journal of Finance*, 45, 455-477.

La Porta, R., J. Lakonishok, A. Shleifer, and R. Vishny, 1997, "Good News for Value Stocks: Further Evidence on Market Efficiency," *The Journal of Finance*, 52, 859-874.

Latané, H. and C. Jones, 1977, "Standardized Unexpected Earnings – A Progress Report," *The Journal of Finance*, 32, 1457-1465.

Lehmann, B., 1990, "Fads, Martingales, and Market Efficiency," *Quarterly Journal of Economics*, 105, 1-28.

Lehmann, B. and D. Modest, 1987, "Mutual Fund Performance Evaluation: A Comparison of Benchmarks and Benchmark Comparisons," *The Journal of Finance*, 42, 233-265.

Liu, P., S. Smith, and A. Syed, 1990, "Stock Price Reactions to *The Wall Street Journal*'s Securities Recommendations," *Journal of Financial and Quantitative Analysis*, 25, 399-410.

Loughran, T. and J. Ritter, 1995, "The New Issues Puzzle," *The Journal of Finance*, 50, 23-52.

Loughran, T. and J. Ritter, 1997, "The Operating Performance of Firms Conducting Seasoned Equity Offerings," *The Journal of Finance*, 52, 1823-1850.

Lunde, A., A. Timmermann, and D. Blake, 1999, "The Hazards of Mutual Fund Underperformance: A Cox Regression Analysis," *Journal of Empirical Finance*, 6, 121-152.

MacKinlay, A., 1995, "Multifactor Models Do Not Explain Deviations from the CAPM," *Journal of Financial Economics*, 38, 3-28.

Malkiel, B., 1995, "Returns from Investing in Equity Mutual Funds: 1971-1991," *The Journal of Finance*, 50, 549-572.

Marsh, T. and R. Merton, 1986, "Dividend Variability and Variance Bounds Tests for the Rationality of Stock Market Prices," *American Economic Review*, 76, 483-498.

Massa, M., 2003, "How Do Family Strategies Affect Fund Performance? When Performance-Maximization Is Not the Only Game in Town," *Journal of Financial Economics*, 67, 249-304.

McConnell, J. and G. Sanger, 1987, "The Puzzle in Post-Listing Common Stock Returns," *The Journal of Finance*, 42, 119-140.

McDonald, J., 1974, "Objectives and Performance of Mutual Funds, 1960-1969," *Journal of Financial and Quantitative Analysis*, 9, 311-333.

McLeod, R. and D. Malhotra, 1994, "A Re-examination of the Effect of 12-b-1 Plans on Mutual Fund Expense Ratios," *The Journal of Financial Research*, 17, 231-240.

Mendenhall, R., 1991, "Evidence of Possible Underweighting of Earnings-Related Information," *Journal of Accounting Research*, 29, 170-180.

Michaely, R., R. Thaler, and K. Womack, 1995, "Price Reactions to Dividend Initiations and Omissions: Overreaction or Drift?," *The Journal of Finance*, 50, 573-608.

Michaely, R. and K. Womack, 1999, "Conflict of Interest and the Credibility of Underwriter Analyst Recommendations," *Review of Financial Studies*, 12, 653-686.

Miller, T. and N. Gressis, 1980, "Nonstationarity and Evaluation of Mutual Fund Performance," *Journal of Financial and Quantitative Analysis*, 15, 639-654.

Morningstar Mutual Funds, 2002, Chicago: Morningstar, Inc.

Nanda, V., Z. Wang, and L. Zheng, 2004, "Family Values and the Star Phenomenon: Strategies of Mutual Fund Families," *Review of Financial Studies*, 17, 667-698.

National Association of Securities Dealers, 2001, Manual, Chicago: CCH Incorporated.

Odean, T., 1998, "Are Investors Reluctant to Realize Their Losses," *The Journal of Finance*, 53, 1775-1798.

Odean, T., 1998, "Volume, Volatility, Price, and Profits When All Traders Are Above Average," *The Journal of Finance*, 53, 1887-1934.

Odean, T., 1999, "Do Investors Trade Too Much?," *American Economic Review*, 89, 1279-1298.

Oesterle, D., D. Winslow, and S. Anderson, 1992, "The New York Stock Exchange and Its Out Moded Specialist System: Can the Exchange Innovate to Survive?," *The Journal of Corporation Law*, 2, 223-310.

Pastor, L. and R. Stambaugh, 2002, "Investing in Equity Mutual Funds," *Journal of Financial Economics*, 63, 351-380.

Pastor, L. and R. Stambaugh, 2002, "Mutual Fund Performance and Seemingly Unrelated Assets," *Journal of Financial Economics*, 63, 315-349.

Poser, N., 1984, "Options Account Fraud: Securities Churning in a New Context," *The Business Lawyer*, 39, 571-615.

Poterba, J. and L. Summers, 1988, "Mean Reversion in Stock Returns: Evidence and Implications," *Journal of Financial Economics*, 22, 27-59.

Prather, L. and K. Middleton, 2002, "Are N + 1 Heads Better than One? The Case of Mutual Fund Managers," *Journal of Economic Behavior & Organization*, 47, 103-120.

Reinganum, M., 1983, "The Anomalous Stock Market Behavior of Small Firms in January: Empirical Tests for Tax-Loss Selling Effects," *Journal of Financial Economics*, 12, 89-104.

Richards, A., 1997, "Winner-Loser Reversals in National Stock Market Indices: Can They Be Explained?," *The Journal of Finance*, 52, 2129-2144.

Richards, R., D. Fraser, and J. Groth, 1980, "Winning Strategies for Closed-End Funds," *Journal of Portfolio Management*, 7, 50-55.

Rouwenhorst, K., 1998a, "International Momentum Strategies," *The Journal of Finance*, 53, 267-284.

Rouwenhorst, K., 1998b, "Local Return Factors and Turnover in Emerging Stock Markets," *The Journal of Finance*, 54, 139-164.

Rozeff, M. and M. Zaman, 1988, "Market efficiency and insider trading; New evidence," *Journal of Business*, 61, 25-44.

Sapp, T. and A. Tiwari, 2004, "Does Stock Return Momentum Explain the 'Smart Money' Effect?," *The Journal of Finance*, 59, 2605-2622.

Schabacker, R., 1930, *Stock Market Theory and Practice*, New York: Forbes Publishing.

Schlarbaum, G., W. Lewellen, and R. Lease, 1978a, "The Common-Stock-Portfolio Performance Record of Individual Investors: 1964-70," *The Journal of Finance*, 33, 429-441.

Schlarbaum, G., W. Lewellen, and R. Lease, 1978b, "Realized Returns on Common Stock Investments: The Experience of Individual Investors," *Journal of Business*, 51, 299-325.

SEC Website: Securities and Exchange Commission, Investor Complaints and Questions, 2002, accessed January, 2003. http://www.sec.gov.

Seyhun, H., "1986, Insiders' Profits, Costs of Trading, and Market Efficiency," *Journal of Financial Economics*, 61, 189-212.

Seyhun, H., 1988, "The Information Content of Aggregate Insider Trading," *Journal of Business*, 61, 1-24.

Seyhun, H., 1997, *Investment Intelligence: Tips from Insider Trading*, Cambridge: MIT Press.

Sharpe, W., 1966, "Mutual Fund Performance," *The Journal of Business*, 39, 119-138.

Sharpe, W., 1992, "Asset Allocation: Management Style and Performance Measurement," *The Journal of Portfolio Management*, Winter, 7-19.

Shefrin, H. and M. Statman, 1985, "The Disposition to Sell Winners Too Early and Ride Losers Too Long: Theory and Evidence," *The Journal of Finance*, 40, 777-790.

Shiller, R., 1981, "Do Stock Prices Move Too Much to be Justified by Subsequent Changes in Dividends?," *American Economic Review*, 71, 421-498.

Shiller, R., 1989, *Market Volatility*, Cambridge: MIT Press.

Sias, R., 1997, "Optimum Trading Strategies for Closed-End Funds." *Journal of Investing*, 6, 54-61.

Snigaroff, R., 2000, "The Economics of Active Management," *The Journal of Portfolio Management*, 26, 16-24.

Spiess, D. and J. Affleck-Graves, 1995, "Underperformance in Long-Run Stock Returns Following Seasoned Equity Offerings," *Journal of Financial Economics*, 38, 243-268.

Statman, M., 2000, "Socially Responsible Mutual Funds," *Financial Analysts Journal*, 3, 30-39.

Stein, A., 2005, "Looking beyond the NYSE," CNN/Money, accessed December, 2005, http://www.money.cnn.com.

Teoh, S., I. Welch, and T. Wong, 1998, "Earnings Management and the Underperformance of Seasoned Equity Offerings," *Journal of Financial Economics*, 50, 63-69.

ter Horst, J., T. Nijman, and M. Verbeek, 2001, "Eliminating Look-Ahead Bias in Evaluating Persistence in Mutual Fund Performance," *Journal of Empirical Finance*, 8, 345-373.

ter Horst, J. and M. Verbeek, 2000, "Estimating Short-Run Persistence in Mutual Fund Performance, *Review of Economics and Statistics*, 82, 646-655.

Treynor, J., 1965, "How to Rate Management of Investment Funds," *Harvard Business Review*, 43, 63-75.

Treynor, J. and K. Mazuy, 1966, "Can Mutual Funds Outguess the Market?," *Harvard Business Review*, July, 131-136.

Trueman, B., 1988, "A Theory of Noise Trading in Security Markets," *The Journal of Finance*, 43, 83-95.

Veit, E. and J. Cheney, 1982, "Are Mutual Funds Market Timers?," *The Journal of Portfolio Management*, Winter, 35-42.

Volkman, D., 1999, "Market Volatility and Perverse Timing Performance of Mutual Fund Managers," *The Journal of Financial Research*, 22, 449-470.

Wermers, R. and T. Moskowitz, 2000, "Mutual Fund Performance: An Empirical Decomposition into Stock-Picking Talent, Style, Transactions Costs, and Expenses," *The Journal of Finance*, 55, 1655-1703.

Wikinews, 2005, "NYSE To Merge with Archipelago; NASDAQ To Buy Instinet," accessed December, 2005, http://www.en.wikinews.org.

Winslow, D. and S. Anderson, 1990, "A Model for Determining the Excessive Trading Element in Churning Claims," *The North Carolina Law Review*, 68, 327-361.

Womack, K., 1996, "Do Brokerage Analysts' Recommendations Have Investment Value?," *The Journal of Finance*, 51, 137-168.

AUTHOR INDEX

SUBJECT INDEX